CONTENTS

The Institute of International Studies, University of South Carolina gratefully acknowledges the kind permission of:

World Politics to republish:

"Interwar International Relations Research: The American Experience," from Vol. II, October 1949;

"The Teaching of International Relations in the United States," from Vol. XIII, April 1961;

"Frederick Sherwood Dunn and the American Study of International Relations," from Vol. XV, October 1962.

D. Van Nostrand Company, Inc., Princeton, N. J., to republish:

"Theories as Forces in Modern World Politics," from *The Role of Theory in International Relations,* edited by Horace V. Harrison, Copyright 1964.

University of Notre Dame Press to republish:

"The Uses of International Relations Theory," from *Theoretical Aspects of International Relations,* 1959.

The final essay in this collection, "Growing Points in the Study of International Relations," has not been published previously.

FOREWORD

Two decades ago a quarterly journal of International Relations, *World Politics,* was introduced to the scholarly community. Its high standards and its subsequent acceptance as the most important learned journal in International Relations (IR) have owed much to the initial impetus and direction provided by the first Managing Editor, William T. R. Fox. In the first issue Fox's colleague at Yale, Frederick Sherwood Dunn, offered a series of propositions about the scope of International Relations as a field of academic teaching and research. Dunn argued that although IR was "still in an early stage of development and that much of what is talked about under the label scarcely deserves recognition as a legitimate subject of academic concern," nevertheless "events have reinforced the growing conviction that the questions of international relations are much too complex and dangerous to be dealt with any longer as sidelines of existing disciplines."

Professor Fox himself a year later looked back over two decades of American scholarship in IR (in a survey which constitutes the first essay in this volume) and concluded: "Whether international relations has yet 'arrived' as a separate social science discipline is probably as much a matter of debate in 1949 as in 1929. But the trends described have certainly increased the relevance of international relations to the making of public policy." In 1968, it is likely that we can repeat this conclusion, but in the interim, IR has become a standard field of teaching and research in major American universities and institutes and the number of International Relationists has grown to the point where they have felt justified in founding their own learned society, the International Studies Association, which meets both regionally and nationally in annual coventions.

It is important for those who embark upon a career in IR, or for that matter those who enter the field simply as a part of liberal arts preparation for participation in an increasingly complex world, to have some background information on the development of the study of IR in the United States, for certainly America has provided the intellectual leadership in the development of the field. One possible approach would be to peruse the twenty published volumes of *World Politics.* Another approach is to gather together the essays of W. T. R. Fox, for he has been the most prescient observer of, as well as leader in, the development of IR studies in America.

The student who worked through all the issues of *World Politics* would undoubtedly agree with Professor Fox's observation (in the last essay which is printed for the first time in this volume) that "Approaches to the study of international relations have in the first two-thirds of the twentieth century generally been cumulative . . . the newer types of international relations research have in each period ordinarily complemented but not displaced the older. Ours is an expanding and not merely a changing subject."

The past two decades have witnessed various vogues and thrusts in teaching and publication in IR. Earlier foci of maximum interest, such as concentration on power, or geopolitical determinants of policy, are now taken for granted or form the foundations for other emphases. Attention has swung from a concentration on the decision making process in foreign policy to the nature and role of national character or national style, to elite studies, to comparative foreign policy systems, to comparative studies in modernization, to systems analysis, and to science and the computers for the communications analysts.

Through the course of this development of International Relations study, W. T. R. Fox has been at the center of the stage. It is useful to bring together his essays about the development of IR because he is its best chronicler, but it is also appropriate because his own contributions have been every bit as formidable as the works of other leaders to whom he gives credit. Together with his wife, Annette Baker Fox, who is a distinguished International Relationist in her own right and who frequently co-authors works with him (as is the case in the second essay in this volume), he has authored several significant volumes in the IR field. His writing always exhibits the utmost of care and precision. He is, in many respects, a scholar's scholar, and for this reason, as each of the following essays demonstrates, Fox can frequently pack more into an article for a learned journal than others put between the covers of a book.

Perhaps an even more formidable contribution which Professor Fox has made in the field of International Relations has been in his role as a teacher. Few have been as generous with their time or as painstaking in assistance to graduate students. The scores who have participated in his seminars and enjoyed the rigorous quality of academic discussion and idea-testing upon which he always insists, are presently the leaders in the IR field in the United States and abroad, and many others hold or have held positions of high responsibility in the actual conduct of American foreign policy.

W. T. R. Fox received a B.S. degree from Haverford College and subsequently studied at the University of Chicago where he received his doctorate in 1940, a time when Chicago was preeminent among the centers of International Relations study in the United States. Subsequently, after having taught at Temple University and Princeton University, he moved to Yale where he was one of the key members of that talented group who created the Institute of International Studies at Yale and initiated publication of *World Politics*. In 1950, Professor Fox accepted an appointment as Professor of International Relations at Columbia University and the following year was named Director of the Institute of War and Peace Studies there. In subsequent years he has continued to inspire and assist younger scholars in IR, has served in a consultant capacity with private and governmental organizations, and has participated in conferences at home and abroad.

It is surely fitting that the Institute of International Studies at the University of South Carolina should publish this collection of Professor Fox's essays. Four members of the staff of the Institute, including the undersigned, have been his students, and the Institute's program has drawn much inspiration and advice from him. We are convinced that students of IR will benefit greatly from an opportunity to read the essays of W. T. R. Fox gathered between the covers of one book in much the same manner as we have benefited from his guidance and instruction in the growing International Relations field whose problems and prospects he describes so well.

RICHARD L. WALKER,
James F. Byrnes Professor of
International Relations.

Columbia, South Carolina,
January 12, 1968.

I

INTERWAR INTERNATIONAL RELATIONS RESEARCH: THE AMERICAN EXPERIENCE[1]

From *World Politics,* Vol. II, October, 1949

What is today in the United States conventionally known as international relations is a subject different in content and emphasis from its counterpart of even two decades ago. Much of what seemed important in 1929 seems irrelevant, and some of it even trivial, in 1949. Another twenty years may perhaps bring a similar judgment on work now being done. But we ought at least to be aware of the direction in which we have been moving if we are to control the future development of the field.

In 1930 the following statement passed unchallenged in a discussion among some of America's leading social scientists: "The emotional drive is so highly developed in the kind of person who goes into the international relations field that it often leads to unclear thinking." The implication that no one without this drive could conceivably be persuaded to enter the field is a commentary on the disesteem with which international relations research was then regarded.

---

[1] This essay was originally prepared for the Committee on International Relations Research of the Social Science Research Council. The Committee had as its chairman Frederick S. Dunn, then Director of the Institute of International Studies at Yale University. I was its secretary. The essay was published in the October, 1949, issue of *World Politics,* along with a companion piece by Professor Dunn, "The Present Course of International Relations Research."—W. T. R. F.

The desire for legitimacy, for recognition as a scholar by the community of scholars, has been a powerful spur to soul-searching activity. An even more compelling reason has been the failure of events in the 1930's to accord with the expectations generated by the academic study of international relations in the 1920's. From the invasion of Manchuria to the signing of the Molotov-Ribbentrop agreement, students of international relations too often found themselves emotionally and intellectually unprepared for the event. If they are to be taken seriously in the 1950's, they must show that they now know what went wrong, that they now know what sorts of data and analysis would have given them in the 1930's the answers that were then denied them.

I

Interest in America in the study of international relations seems to have been generated by the old nineteenth-century peace movement. The first effect of this on the academic world was an increased emphasis on international law, largely because of the central place which arbitration then occupied in plans for eliminating war.

The early years of the twentieth century saw the establishment of such institutions as the World Peace Foundation and the Carnegie Endowment for International Peace. To Mr. Ginn, the publisher, and Mr. Carnegie, the steelmaker, the gentlemen responsible for establishing these organizations, it seemed quite possible that with a little extra intellectual effort and a little greater missionary zeal the evil of war could be abolished. Both Mr. Ginn and Mr. Carnegie entertained high hopes for early success in abolishing this "foulest blot upon our high civilization." Carnegie even went so far as to direct Trustees of the Carnegie Endowment for International Peace, as follows:

> When . . . war is discarded as disgraceful to civilized men, the Trustees will pleas then consider what is the next most degrading evil or evils whose banishment—or what new elevating element or elements if introduced or fostered, or both combined—would most advance the progress, elevation and happiness of man, and so on from century to century without end, my Trustees of each age shall determin how they can best aid man in his upward march to higher and higher stages of development unceasingly; for now we know that man was created not with an instinct for his own degradation, but imbued with the desire and the

power for improvement to which, perchance, there may be no limit short of perfection even here in this life upon earth.[2]

The men most influential in giving shape to college, university, and research organization work in the field of international relations between the two World Wars grew up under the influence of the ideology which motivated Mr. Ginn and Mr. Carnegie to establish their respective peace organizations. They did not all share Mr. Carnegie's belief that the world could be won for peace in our time by using the techniques of the old-time revival meeting. Such a conception indeed repelled such coldly intellectual persons as Elihu Root. But they did believe that the final elimination of war was a much more simple matter than their counterparts of today believe.

Why could permanent peace seem to be an attainable short-run objective in the early years of our century? Especially in the United States, war was thought of as a procedure for settling disputes to which rational men would resort only if other procedures were unavailable. Many, to be sure, recognized that this formula would never account for the wars of a Napoleon or a Bismarck. But they believed that the trend of history was toward free government and that a free constitutional democratic people would never permit its government to embark on wars of aggression. The recipe for peace was therefore simple: democracy, international understanding, and arbitration.

The triumphant spread of constitutional democracy was apparently taken for granted. No endowments or foundations of comparable size were set up to promote the spread of democratic institutions. The firmly established tradition of non-intervention would in any case have inhibited the growth of a popular movement to abolish the evil of absolutism. It seemed a contradiction in terms to think of imposing democratic institutions on countries not yet able to produce from within themselves a revolutionary democratic leadership.

To the assumption of the inevitable spread of free institutions, at least among the areas of European culture and inheritance, was often added the assumption of a basic harmony of interests. Why did not this underlying harmony of interests between peoples lead to a final elimination of war? The answer, it was thought, was two-

[2] Mr. Carnegie's letter to the Trustees read at their first meeting, December 14, 1910. *Year Book for 1911,* Carnegie Endowment for International Peace, Washington, D. C., 1912, p. 3. Andrew Carnegie was a believer in simplified spelling.

fold: lack of understanding and lack of procedures. The peace foundations accordingly set themselves the two tasks of promoting international intercourse and of discovering new ways of achieving the pacific settlement of international disputes.

To promote international intercourse was to hasten the development of the international mind which would find war as irrational and anachronistic as trial by ordeal. In this situation, past experience seemed to have little to teach. It had only produced recurrent wars, and war was to be abolished. With the development of the international mind the underlying harmony of interests was expected to become apparent. Peace then would only be a matter of having available proper procedures for pacific settlement.

The fifteen years before the First World War were periods of great inventiveness in the area of pacific settlement of international disputes. The Department of State was run by lawyers; each dispute was regarded as a case; and men like Root and Carnegie could agree on the importance of expanding the use of arbitration. This is the period of the two Hague Peace Conferences. It is the period of the Bryan "cooling off" treaties. When governments actually came to the point of negotiating general arbitration treaties, they did not reflect completely the optimism of the proponents of arbitration or other forms of pacific settlement. They always left an escape hatch in the agreement to arbitrate. Thus, vital interests, independence, and honor were often three excepted categories. Since these are the elastic categories into which a dispute leading to war almost always seems to fall, the elaboration of arbitration treaties apparently averted no wars. Certainly the world conflagration of 1914-18 proved that here was no sure way to eliminate war.

Four years of war disillusioned those who thought that peace was simply a matter of having available the right sort of procedures. To the prewar trinity of democracy, international understanding, and arbitration was added national self-determination, disarmament, and collective security. But the pre-World War I interest in form rather than function remained.

The old system was thought of as absolutely bad. It was in even worse repute than in 1914 when it had not yet produced the First World War. It had no lessons to teach and there was remarkably little analysis of the political function which would still have to be performed in a reorganized state system. The historian in this respect frequently had little more to offer than the political scientist. The tremendous research effort on war guilt seemed only to document the badness of the diplomats and their system and to contribute little to understanding the causes of war and conditions of peace.[3]

The political scientist's focus on form rather than function meant detailed consideration of the forms of the supposedly emerging world commonwealth. The international political process as it was then operating was viewed as a regrettable, but one hoped short-lived, survival from the bad old days.[4]

II

The activities of the Social Science Research Council's various international relations committees exemplify the prevailing attitude both of those social scientists working in the field and of those outside it.[5] Professor James T. Shotwell referred in a 1927 report to "new forms arising which if they mature will modify the entire relationship of civilized nations." [6] These new forms, it was said, "cannot be studied adequately by instruments at our disposal." The reference to "new forms" was of course to the Geneva institutions.

Intensive study of League activities apparently was believed to dispose of the "political" aspect of international relations. There were also economic, social, and legal "aspects" to be studied, but

[3] The search by the historian for *the* person or persons responsible for bringing on World War I was paralleled by other social scientists' quest for *the* cause of war. Various simplistic determinisms, other than those already alluded to, among which economic determinism and the devil theory of war were probably the most fashionable, flourished. In a way the belief in the possibility of discovering *the* cause of war reflected the prevailing optimism; for if the cause could be isolated, the cure could be prescribed.

[4] Concentration on the Geneva institutions was most highly developed in the United States but was not a unique characteristic of the American student of international relations. Professor S. H. Bailey in England was able to interpret a directive to survey educational and research activities "in so far as they tend to impart a knowledge of the League and develop a spirit of international co-operation" as a mandate to survey "the objective study of international relations." See his *International Studies in Modern Education,* London, 1938.

[5] The SSRC's major effort in the international relations field in the interwar period occurred between 1931 and 1933. Professor James T. Shotwell directed its work as a member of the SSRC staff, and a committee of men of affairs under Owen D. Young replaced the Council's earlier academic international relations committee. The work during this period of concentrated activity was not so much concerned with inquiries into the nature of the field as with the survey of existing organizations and creation of new research organizations here and abroad. His work therefore stands largely outside the scope of the present analysis of trends in research.

[6] "Report of the Advisory Committee on International Relations of the Social Science Research Council," mimeographed, 1927.

there is no clear conception to suggest what the various studies would be aspects of.

It was said at one point that the distinctive characteristic of international relations problems was that they tended to be interdisciplinary.[7] But what the second discipline was did not in the case of most proposed studies appear in the record. What seemed to give a proposed study an international character was that it should involve collection of data from more than one country. Thus "land utilization forms in the Far East" could be and was approved as a study worthy of support as an international relations project; land utilization forms in Siam—or any other one country—presumably would not have been.

Land utilization forms may well be of great interest to students of world politics. But this might be so even if all the important data could be studied in one country. Whatever criterion should be adopted in selecting projects for research, the number of states from which data is to be collected is not such a criterion.

A similar question-begging formula for dealing with international relations research was evolved in the mid-thirties. In 1936 a reconstituted Social Science Research Council committee expressed itself in favor of what was called the "segmental approach." Robert Crane, then Director of the Council, supported this view. He asserted that it was "impossible to treat research in international relations as a unit." Their suggestion was that in accordance with the segmental approach work should begin on the economic side. Again there was no particular indication as to the economic side of what. Mr. Crane may well be right as to the lack of unity of international relations research, but it by no means follows that all important international relations projects could be fitted into then existing categories. Neither those who asserted the unity of the subject and the utility of recognizing it as a separate discipline nor the academic detractors of the subject seem to have left any place for international politics. This remained largely in the domain of the historian.

The records of the Social Science Research Council's various international relations committees at no time show any sustained effort to set up criteria for determining which researches should be supported. Given adequate financial support there were few projects recommended or even suggested which could not have been

[7] *Ibid.*

studied by methods already at the disposal of social science. Securing adequate financial support is not a minor matter, but there are few working in the field today who wish to think of the label "international relations" as simply a "come-on" device in dealing with potential donors.

III

The account of research in the interwar period has so far emphasized the role of a particular institution designed to promote research. But research is performed by individuals and not by committees seeking to promote research. Any judgment on the interwar experience in international relations research should rest upon the publications of individual scholars. Such men as the following were occupying the chief international relations professorships in political science departments during the interwar period—David P. Barrows, Clarence A. Berdahl, Philip Marshall Brown, Kenneth Colegrove, Frederick S. Dunn, Charles G. Fenwick, James Garner, Ralston Hayden, Amos Hershey, Charles P. Howland, Charles Cheney Hyde, Parker T. Moon, Roland Morris, DeWitt C. Poole, Pitman Potter, Harold Quigley, Jesse S. Reeves, Frank M. Russell, James T. Shotwell, Nicholas J. Spykman, Graham Stuart, W. W. Willoughby, George Grafton Wilson, and Quincy Wright. The list is representative rather than complete and includes only men who had been appointed to professorships by 1930.

Their research is to a notable degree characterized by high technical competence and lack of chauvinism. Much of their research which has proved of great importance to the field could be and was completed without any special international relations technique having to be developed. This was especially true in the areas of international law and organization and the conduct of foreign relations, the fields of specialization of eighteen of the twenty-four men listed above. The same observations could be made about the research carried on by the diplomatic historian, the student of international economic policy, and the law school professor of international law.[8]

What were the attitudes and beliefs which influenced the character of the contribution which most of those in the political science

[8] See, for example, the works directed or edited or written by such men as Shotwell (the series on the economic and social history of the First World War), Fay and Schmitt (the war guilt studies), Hayes and Moon (on nationalism and imperialism), Merriam (the civic training series), and Hudson (the codification of international law).

profession could make to the new study of international relations? The traditional emphasis on international law was maintained, but there were other orientations more specifically associated with the interwar period, orientations which men like John Bassett Moore for example did not share.

There was a tendency to equate "peace" and "government" on the one hand and "war" and "power politics" on the other. Research was therefore strongly oriented toward international government. The typical political scientist, who in domestic politics regarded the study of government and the study of political science as identical, projected this conception onto the international scene. International politics was left to the historian and he was often preoccupied with discovering the villain in the piece.

Just as it took the bitter experience of the interwar period to dramatize the fact that democratic institutions would not automatically flourish once democratic constitutions had been adopted, so it took the breakdown of the Versailles order to make clear how much more there is to creating a world commonwealth than drafting its charter. The study of international organization has gained rather than lost urgency but emphasis is shifting to analyzing the political conditions necessary for its development.

The usually unexamined assumption that everything international was better than anything national biased the selection of research projects. Since peace and the various new proposals for insuring its perpetual maintenance seemed so obviously to be a good thing, subjects like disarmament and pacific settlement were, as isolated problems, disproportionately overstudied. So were "good" international things like collective security and peaceful change and "bad" national things like nationalist attitudes, imperialism, and the munitions makers. There was a corresponding underemphasis on "bad" international things like the Third International and "good" national things like American security. The national interests which the new international institutions were expected to protect and the ways by which these values should be protected if the new international institutions were not by themselves adequate for the job were on the whole neglected. It was thus partly traditional definitions of political science and partly culturally determined normative inhibitions which channeled research effort away from studying the politics of the contemporary state system.

Although the First World War had rudely shaken men's faith in the inevitability of progress, it was still fashionable to believe in an underlying harmony of interest which with a little more education would become apparent to men of good will in every country. Knowledge was thus held to be an automatic and sure guarantee of understanding.[9] It took Hitler and the Second World War to disillusion many men who had continued to believe that "truth" alone would reveal to men everywhere their underlying harmony of interests.

It is no doubt true that rational men equipped with what most Americans would consider socially acceptable sets of value preferences would find it difficult to discover a situation in which international war is a paying proposition for either the victor or the vanquished. Even before the First World War, Sir Norman Angell had convincingly developed "the case for peace" on rational grounds. The illusion under which Sir Norman Angell labored when in 1910 he wrote his *The Great Illusion*[10] was that he was writing for a world of rational men, equipped with value systems like his own, who were evenly distributed on the two sides of every international frontier. He did not deal with the case of a nation of rational men, sharing his values, who find themselves attacked. Would it be worthwhile for them to try to win on the theory that the vanquished loses even more than the victor? How much a unilateral increase in understanding makes for peace is something which ought to be examined rather than assumed.

For present purposes, what is important about the unexamined assumption of an underlying harmony of interests and the equating of peace and "understanding" is that it diverted energy and resources which might otherwise have gone into genuine research. An attempt to make the implicit harmony explicit by promotion of international understanding and other activities which are essentially irrelevant in terms of their contribution to human knowledge, however valuable they may be in other ways, absorbed much of these energies and resources. In fact the hard intellectual task involved in discovering the conditions under which national interests could be harmonized was rarely undertaken. The job to be done was to prescribe the conditions of harmonization not to assert the fact of harmony.[11]

---

[9] Some of the more exaggerated claims made about UNESCO's contribution to maintaining world peace suggest that this belief still persists.

[10] New York, G. P. Putnam's Sons, 1910.

[11] Cf. Walter Lippmann, *An Inquiry into the Principles of the Good Society*, Boston, Little, Brown, 1937, for an analogous description of what went wrong with *laissez-faire* economics.

Those who did not accept the League of Nations focus for the subject frequently found themselves in a difficult predicament. Their lack of focus reinforced the tendency to regard international relations more and more as a highfalutin way of studying current events. One thing which the international relationists could do which the historian was not already doing would be to deal with the recent events which the historian shied away from recounting. Here was a function which somebody ought to perform; the international relationists leaped happily into the breach. A leap into this particular breach was unhappily a leap away from applying the analytical skills of the social sciences to solving the problems of war and peace.

In the absence of a sharply defined focus, the international relationist who rejected current history as his peculiar province has no generally accepted, scientific criteria for the selection of research projects. "General worth-whileness" and availability of data were the only two criteria developed. Neither of these criteria is in itself bad, but in the absence of any other criteria of relevance they tend to discourage efforts to put a given research into a scientifically meaningful frame of reference. The second criterion, availability of data, explains the heavy concentration of research in the four fields of international law, international organization, international trade and finance, and diplomatic history. These were the four subareas in the field with profuse documentation. That intensive study in these fields had ultimate relevance to basic problems of war and peace cannot be doubted. What the relevance of particular research projects to the basic study of how men could live together more peaceably was rarely examined. Thus even the studies in these four fields were provincial in the sense that a problem in international law was treated as contributing to the solution of another problem in international law, etc. There was occasional testimony to the important contribution which the psychologists, the anthropologists, the sociologists could make to the study of international relations but the nature of this contribution was rarely examined.

In summary, one could say that the analytical model used for investigative purposes was a world commonwealth characterized by permanent peace. The real world was described in terms of its deviation from this model. In the collection of data, on the other hand, there was a high devotion to the use of empirical techniques in areas where there was a wealth of data but a great timidity about extending or combining the areas in which hypotheses are to be tested by empirical research.

IV

The pattern just described is of course not characteristic of the whole body of academic research during the period between the two wars and it is less characteristic of research at the end of the period than of that at the beginning. Whether from Marx or from Machiavelli, from European geopolitics or American war debunking, from German sociology or Columbia historians, or from a change in the intellectual climate of American social science, generally, a new realism and a new interest in group interests—national, transnational, and subnational—was increasingly felt. Studies which interrelated the domestic and international political process became more frequent.

Charles A. Beard, for example, was raising questions about national interest. He was writing as early as 1930 "I want to know what the devil it really is." That Beard got what many would today consider the wrong answers is less important than that he asked the right question.[12]

The same year saw the opening of the Walter Hines Page School at Johns Hopkins whose stated purpose was "to create a research laboratory for the study of the motivating causes of the conduct of nations in relation to one another." Frederick S. Dunn's various books between 1929 and 1933 are one product of that laboratory.[13] The interest in the behavior of diplomats and in the decision-making process which he then exhibited has since become more fashionable.

At Chicago the Causes of War Study under Quincy Wright was by then well under way and the two-volume *A Study of War*[14] which was completed a decade later stands as a monument to a research effort which focused on an existing political institution rather than on some future utopia.

Frederick Schuman's *International Politics*[15] sought to describe an existing state system rather than a future world commonwealth. Harold Lasswell's *World Politics and Personal Insecurity*[16] is in terms of the prevailing academic environment for international rela-

---

[12] See *The Idea of National Interest,* New York, Macmillan, 1934; and *The Open Door at Home,* New York, Macmillan, 1934.

[13] See *The Practice and Procedure of International Conferences,* Baltimore, The Johns Hopkins Press, 1929; *The Protection of Nationals,* Baltimore, The Johns Hopkins Press, 1932; and *The Diplomatic Protection of Americans in Mexico,* New York, Columbia University Press, 1933.

[14] Chicago, University of Chicago Press, 1942.

[15] 1st edition, New York, McGraw-Hill, 1933.

[16] New York, McGraw-Hill, 1935.

tions research a work of great precocity. Its tone and focus is in most ways more congenial to the intellectual atmosphere of the 1940's than to that of the interwar period.

Edward Mead Earle,[17] Harold and Margaret Sprout,[18] and Nicholas J. Spykman[19] are notable for their rediscovery of national security problems and for focusing their research upon them. Arnold Wolfers in his *Britain and France between Two Wars*[20] led the way in systematically relating the activities at Geneva to the foreign policies and national interests of the great powers and these in turn to the ideologies of the major political groupings within each country.

A body of political theory dealing with a system characterized by an absence of central authority has yet to be developed, but its rudiments are found in the works of some of these men.[21] In their work and elsewhere two perspectives on world politics uncharacteristic of the 1920's became increasingly important thereafter.

1. International politics is moved to the focus and other subjects are related to it. With politics at the center, it becomes possible to help the anthropologist, for example, ask the right questions. International organization is studied in a political, and not a predominantly constitutional, context. International politics can then deal with all group interests which influence politics in a world of nation-states and not just with official interstate relationships.

2. In their scholarly capacity political scientists neither affirmed nor denied the legitimacy of national interests on *a priori* grounds and just because the interest was national. There was, however, recognition that the interests which governments are trying to promote must be identified, as must various transnational and subnational group interests. This is an absolute prerequisite to useful research on the problem of harmonizing the various national interests so that a broader supranational community of interest can more easily develop.

---

[17] See his "National Security and Foreign Policy," *Yale Review*, Spring, 1940, pp. 444-60; and "Political and Military Strategy for the United States," *Proceedings of the Academy of Political Science*, January, 1941, pp. 112-19.

[18] See Harold and Margaret Sprout, *The Rise of American Naval Power, 1776-1918*, Princeton, Princeton University Press, 1939; *Toward a New Order of Sea Power*, Princeton, Princeton University Press, 1940.

[19] See *America's Strategy in World Politics*, New York, Harcourt, Brace, 1942.

[20] New York, Harcourt, Brace, 1940.

[21] Grayson L. Kirk reaches a similar conclusion in *The Study of International Relations*, New York, Council on Foreign Relations, 1947.

Whether international relations has yet "arrived" as a separate social science discipline is probably as much a matter of debate in 1949 as in 1929. But the trends described have certainly increased the relevance of international relations research to the making of public policy.

II

THE TEACHING OF INTERNATIONAL RELATIONS IN THE UNITED STATES

From *World Politics*, Vol. XIII, April, 1961 *

International relations, as a subject of instruction, has flourished more in the United States than elsewhere and more in recent years than ever before. What forces explain its growth and its present shape? How have methods of teaching it been affected by the goals of the teacher, by his relation to research, and by the formal organization of international studies in American colleges and universities? To what extent is the American experience so rooted in uniquely American conditions that it is unlikely to be repeated elsewhere? These questions will be considered in turn.

I

Professor Alfred Grosser, in a penetrating review of a number of international relations works of ambitious scope, has asked if the study of international relations is not an American specialty.[1] Ameri-

* This essay was first published in *International Relations in the University* (London, Atlantic Treaty Association, 1960). The version published in *World Politics,* Vol. XIII, 1961, was slightly revised.

[1] "L'étude des relations internationales, spécialité américaine?" *Revue Française de Science Politique,* vi. No. 3 (July-September 1956), pp. 634-51. Quincy Wright, *The Study of International Relations* (New York, Appleton Century Crofts, 1955) and Hans Morgenthau, *Politics Among Nations* (2nd ed., New York, Alfred A. Knopf, 1954), are reviewed at length. There are briefer comments on seven general textbooks.

cans who are teaching, researching, and publishing in the field of international relations are so numerous and so ubiquitous that it is not easy to escape that impression.[2] There are about twenty general textbooks on international relations of American origin currently in print. In addition to *Foreign Affairs* and the specialized journals, *International Organization, American Journal of International Law,* and those devoted to the problems of particular geographic areas, there are three journals primarily addressed to the professional student of international relations: *Journal of Conflict Resolution, Orbis,* and *World Politics.*

The American study of international relations reflects a "voluntaristic" attitude toward questions of foreign policy: a belief that Americans can, by the foreign policy choices they make, be masters of their own destiny.[3] Arnold Wolfers, writing about the attitude in our handling of foreign affairs, has described an Anglo-American "philosophy of choice," which he contrasts with a Continental European "philosophy of necessity."[4] It certainly used to be true that insular location, a naval defensive screen, and great war potential combined, prior to our own century, to permit Britain and the United States a genuine freedom to maintain low levels of peacetime defense mobilization, to eschew defensive alliances, and to postpone both decisions to intervene in European wars and decisions to mobilize to make that intervention effective. In this former era of insularity, American students of international relations could write in time of peace as if the imperatives of national security set

[2] Much of the ferment, vigor, and variety, however, in the American study of international relations has come from men whose origin and, in many cases, entire scholarly training were European. It was not only in atomic physics that the traumatic European events of the 1930's and the beckoning opportunities in the United States combined to make it easier for many scholars to go to America than to go to another European country. John Herz, Hans Kelsen, Hans Morgenthau, Sigmund Neumann, Stefan Possony, Hans Speier, Nicholas Spykman, Robert Strausz-Hupé, and Arnold Wolfers had all put down new roots in American soil before World War II. Postwar appointments at Harvard of Stanley Hoffman, at Yale of Karl Deutsch, at Notre Dome of Stephen Kertesz, and at American University of Michael Lindsay are demonstrations of a continuing receptivity to scholars of transtlantic origin.

[3] Reinhold Niebuhr has attributed "the error of excessive voluntarism" to those who assume that "it would be a fairly easy achievement for nations to abridge their sovereignty in favor of a new international authority" (*The Children of Light and the Children of Darkness,* New York, Scribner's, 1944, p. 169). Voluntarism can also be "excessive" in a nationalist direction, as was shown by the emotion-charged debate as to which Americans brought about the loss of mainland China to the Communists. Presumably, there is a degree of voluntarism which Professor Niebuhr would not regard as excessive.

[4] "Political Theory and International Relations," introductory essay in Arnold Wolfers and Laurence W. Martin, eds., *The Anglo-American Tradition in Foreign Affairs,* New Haven, Yale University Press, 1956, pp. ix-xxvii.

few limits on American freedom of action. Many of them did not view the European "balance of power" state system as a legitimate order to be lived with and adapted to. They saw in that order the focus of infection for the war disease—a disease to be cured or, if that were not possible, to be quarantined.

The great transformations of twentieth-century world politics have drastically changed the focus and content of the typical international relations course without essentially modifying the reformist or, at any rate, meliorist attitudes of the teachers and writers.[5] It is now accepted that loss of insularity has taken away from the American people their freedom to choose to remain aloof from the politics of Europe, Africa, and Asia. There remains, however, the conviction that what the United States does or does not do makes a difference. American professors of international relations, no matter how little policy-oriented their intellectual interests may be, generally believe that deeper and more wide-spread knowledge of international relations will somehow result in better public policies and therefore in a better world for Americans to live in. They now know that even a superpower does not have unlimited choice,[6] but they by no means see the future as wholly predetermined.

A list of these great transformations would include: (1) the expansion of the European state system into a world system, with the superpowers peripheral to Europe playing unprecedented roles in a bipolar system; (2) the diffusion outward from Europe to the Afro-Asian world of nationalism and of demands for rising living standards and the dignity of participation in the political process; (3) the democratization of the control of foreign relations at the same time that the widened sphere of state activity has made the conduct of foreign relations ever more complex and difficult; (4) the sudden emergence of science and technology as great and semi-

[5] The key concept in a notable teaching experiment in international relations at San Francisco State College has been "transformations." Materials compiled and edited for this teaching experiment, and published as "Chandler Studies in International and Intercultural Relations," include three specifically dealing with transformations: Charles A. McClelland, *Nuclear Weapons, Missiles, and Future War*, DeVere E. Pentony, *The Underdeveloped Lands*, and Urban G. Whitaker, Jr., *Nationalism and International Progress*, San Francisco, Calif., Howard Chandler, 1960.

[6] Three members of the State Department's policy-planning staff during the Truman administration subsequently produced books stressing the "realities" and therefore the limits of choice in American foreign policy. See Louis J. Halle, *Dream and Reality*, New York, Harper, 1959; George F. Kennan, *Realities of American Foreign Policy*, Princeton, N. J., Princeton University Press, 1955; Charles B. Marshall, *The Limits of Foreign Policy*, New York, Henry Holt, 1954.

independent variables in the equations of world politics; (5) the drawing-together of the old states of Europe and the transoceanic states of European culture in varying forms of association, such as the European Coal and Steel Community, the British Commonwealth, and NATO; and (6) the new necessity, especially for the superpowers, to do things in peacetime which many states formerly did only in war—maintain a high level of defense mobilization, engage in coalition military planning, finance a massive foreign aid program, and develop a vigorous psychological strategy.

The study of international relations has been reshaped in an effort to clarify American choices as to how to counter, or adapt to, or give direction to these transformations.[7] The bipolar system and the concern for the new policy problems of the Far East, the Middle East, and Africa have caused a tremendous upsurge of area studies. Typical leading American universities have each developed programs for the intensive study of one or more areas formerly thought exotic.[8] There is new interest in regional organization and the conditions under which the leaders of sovereign states most readily permit decisions to be made by regional organizations which the state has joined.[9] There is also an intensified interest in the international social forces which are operating in the turbulent half of the world now in a state of constitutional flux.[10] The inappropriateness of the new instruments of mass destruction for any socially

---

[7] See William Reitzel, Morton A. Kaplan, and Constance G. Coblenz, *United States Foreign Policy,* 1945-1955 (Washington, D. C., Brookings Institution, 1956), for a survey which explicitly relates the relatively unchanging goals of American policy to changing American capabilities and transformations in world politics in order to clarify policy choices made in the decade surveyed and to be made in the years that followed. This was a logical development of Brookings Institution emphasis under Leo Pasvolsky on formulating problems for analysis so that the result would approximate a "position paper" such as might have been prepared inside the Department of State on one of these problems.

[8] Columbia University, for example, has a Russian Institute, an East Asian Institute, and a Near and Middle East Institute. Each has meant a permanent expansion of the faculty by several professorships, and in each case one of the added professors has specialized in the international relations of the area.

[9] *E.g.,* Ernst B. Haas, *The Uniting of Europe,* Stanford, Calif., Stanford University Press, 1958; and Karl W. Deutsch, Sidney A. Burrell, Robert A. Kahn, Maurice Lee, Jr., Martin Lichterman, Raymond E. Lindgren, Francis L. Loewenheim, and Richard W. Van Wagenen, *Political Community and the North Atlantic Area,* Princeton, N. J., Princeton University Press, 1957.

[10] Dankwart Rustow is, for example, an "associate professor of international social forces" at Columbia University. In the Columbia University Bulletin his course of lectures in that subject is described as "a comparative examination of cultural, social, and ideological forces of political change in their international setting. Modernization, nationalism, recruitment of political leadership, the multiplication of sovereignties, and the problems of new states."

acceptable purpose but deterrence has had two quite separate impacts: study by the civilian student of international relations of questions of military strategy and even of pure strategic theory,[11] and a renewed interest in finding technically well-founded bases for arms limitation which would lend added stability to the "balance of terror" and lessen the threat of the accidental or the catalytic war.[12] Finally, with the recognition of the importance of lengthened lead-times in arms production, the enhanced role of force in peace and of limited-war capabilities, and the need for military policies to be continuously coordinated with economic policies and information policies, there is sharply increased attention to national security policy, civil-military relations, and the interplay of domestic and foreign politics.[13]

The American study of international relations has been modified not only in the light of the great transformations of twentieth-century world politics but also in the light of emerging trends and changing fashions in social science, and particularly political science, research. Scholars in international relations have shown the same concern as scholars in domestic politics in endeavoring to make their subject more "scientific,"[14] the same enthusiasm for empirical, behavioral, and quantitative research,[15] the same effort to discover uniformities in state or national behavior,[16] and the same interest

[11] See Bernard Brodie, *Strategy in the Missile Age,* Princeton, N. J., Princeton University Press, 1959; William W. Kaufmann, ed., *Military Policy and National Security,* Princeton, N. J., Princeton University Press, 1956; and Henry A. Kissinger, *Nuclear Weapons and Foreign Policy,* New York, Harper, 1957.

[12] Although the division of labor is not entirely logical, armament policies are usually analyzed in courses on "international politics," while arms limitation policies are dealt with in courses on "international organization." See Joseph Nogee, "The Diplomacy of Disarmament," *International Conciliation,* No. 526 (January 1960); and the symposium issue on "Arms Control" of *Daedalus* (American Academy of Arts and Sciences), Fall 1960.

[13] See, *e.g.,* Samuel P. Huntington, *The Soldier and the State,* Cambridge, Mass., Harvard University Press, 1957; and Walter Millis (with Harvey C. Mansfield and Harold Stein), *Arms and the State,* New York, Twentieth Century Fund, 1958. The Social Science Research Council has for several years had a Committee on National Security Policy Research.

[14] For a discussion of the distinction between scientific and other scholarly writing in international relations and a survey of the former, see Harold D. Lasswell, "The Scientific Study of International Relations," *Yearbook of World Affairs,* xii (1958), pp. 1-28.

[15] See Karl W. Deutsch, *Nationalism and Social Communication,* New York, John Wiley, 1953; and Nathan Leites, "Psycho-Cultural Hypotheses About Political Acts," *World Politics,* I, No. 1 (October, 1948), pp. 102-19.

[16] Thus, Rupert Emerson writes in his preface to *From Empire to Nation: The Rise to Self-Assertion of Asian and African Peoples* (Cambridge, Mass., Harvard University Press, 1960): "I have thrown my scruples to the winds and joined in a search for uniformities on the grand scale." Two recent books

in choosing for investigation problems whose study would clarify questions of public policy.[17] This last interest is not a threat to objectivity so long as the preferences of the disciplined scholar are permitted to operate only in the selection of the problem and not in the mode of observation and analysis.

One development in the postwar study of international relations which has occupied the foreground of the attention of the casual observer has been the so-called "Great Debate" between the realists and the idealists. Pivotal figures on the realist side in this discussion have been Hans J. Morgenthau and his former Chicago colleague, Kenneth W. Thompson.[18] As Dwight Waldo has already commented, *within* the group of international relations and political science scholars, genuine anti-realists are hard to find.[19] "Power" was already enthroned in the 1930's as the central concept in the study of political science at the University of Chicago, where Frederick L. Schuman published the first edition of his pioneering text in 1933[20] and Harold D. Lasswell wrote *World Politics and Personal Insecurity* in 1935.[21] It was equally accepted at Yale, where Nicholas J. Spykman published *America's Strategy in World Politics* in 1942.[22] E. H. Carr's *Twenty Years' Crisis,* which appeared in 1939, enjoyed at least as great a vogue in the United States as in England.[23] Thus, there has been, at least since the 1930's, wide

---

which describe uniformities of state behavior observed in a series of case studies are Annette B. Fox, *The Power of Small States* (Chicago, University of Chicago Press, 1959), and Paul Kecskemeti, *Strategic Surrender* (Stanford, Calif., Stanford University Press, 1958).

[17] *E.g.,* Klaus Knorr, ed., *NATO and American Security,* Princeton, N. J., Princeton University Press, 1959; and Arnold Wolfers, ed., *Alliance Policy in the Cold War,* Baltimore, Md., Johns Hopkins Press, 1956.

[18] Their most recent contributions to the discussion are H. J. Morgenthau, *Dilemmas of Politics,* Chicago, University of Chicago Press, 1958; and K. W. Thompson, *Political Realism and the Crisis of World Politics,* Princeton, N. J., Princeton University Press, 1960.

[19] Dwight Waldo, *Political Science in the United States of America,* Paris, UNESCO, 1956, chap. 5. See William T. R. Fox, "Les fondements moraux et juridiques de la politique étrangère américaine," in *La politique étrangère et ses fondements* (Cahiers de la Fondation Nationale des Sciences Politiques, No. 55, Paris, A. Colin, 1954, pp. 278-90), for a distinction between the doctrinal realist position and what is there called "empirical realism," which is said to characterize most present-day American international relations research. In the idealist-realist debate, Thomas I. Cook and Malcolm Moos (*Power Through Purpose,* Baltimore, Md., Johns Hopkins Press, 1954) are two political scientists on the idealist side.

[20] *International Politics,* New York, McGraw-Hill, 1933.

[21] New York, McGraw-Hill, 1935.

[22] New York, Harcourt Brace, 1942

[23] New York and London, Macmillan, 1939.

acceptance of the proposition that prescriptions for national policy and definitions of the national interest ought to be appropriate for the world we live in rather than for the one we wish we lived in.

Putting "power" rather than "the state" at the center of political science makes it easier to view international relations as one of the political sciences.[24] So conceived, it is possible for some scholars to move effortlessly along the seamless web which connects world politics and the politics of such less inclusive units as the state or the locality, and to emphasize the political process, group behavior, communications studies, conflict resolution, and decision-making.

The nation-states are only contingent units of international relations. The postwar world has seen the emergence of new "bloc actors" in world politics, especially in Western Europe and the North Atlantic community, and new "national actors" with the continued fragmentation of colonial empires. Thus, analysis of the changing group structure of world politics has been one focus of international relations research. Interest in group behavior is not confined, however, to the emergence of new actors. Description and analysis of the behavior of influential elites in the making of foreign policy have been a related interest.[25]

The study of international communications has been something of a specialty of a group now in the Center for International Studies at the Massachusetts Institute of Technology.[26] Conflict resolution has been a unifying concept in the study of international relations at the University of Michigan, where both a journal and a research

[24] The phrase "one of the political sciences" is used in order to avoid discussing whether the study of international relations is or is not a separate discipline and, if it is not, whether it belongs more to political science or to sociology. Certain scholars distinguish between "direct action" and "political action." They reserve the latter term for action taken through or with a view to controlling the action of governments. The study of direct action would lie in the province of sociology and the study of the structure and functioning of international society would be a species of sociology. See N. J. Spykman, *America's Strategy in World Politics,* New York, Harcourt Brace, 1942, p. 13. *The Policy Sciences,* edited by Daniel Lerner and Harold D. Lasswell (Stanford, Calif., Stanford University Press, 1951; translated into French as *Les sciences de la politique aux Etats-Unis,* Paris, A. Colin, 1951), stresses the unity of the studies of which international relations is a part. The content of the study of international relations is not automatically affected by a decision to call it a species of political science, a species of sociology, or something separate from either.

[25] See Gabriel Almond, *The American People and Foreign Policy,* New York, Harcourt Brace, 1950; and Roger Hilsman, "Congressional-Executive Relations and the Foreign Policy Consensus," *American Political Science Review,* LII, No. 3 (September 1958), pp. 725-44.

[26] Cf. Daniel Lerner, *The Passing of Traditional Society,* Glencoe, Ill., Free Press, 1958.

center have been established.[27] Conflicts and their resolution have also been a central theme of students of international organization. The Carnegie Endowment has in course of preparation a series of conflict studies to prepare the way for a comparative analysis, and Leland Goodrich's study of the Korean conflict has clarified the role of the United Nations in this greatest of all efforts to implement the principle of collective security.[28]

A number of not very closely related intellectual efforts are described as having "decision-making" as the focal concept. There is the effort to convey a vicarious sense of participation in the policy-making process by the detailed recreation of a series of events which taken together constituted a "decision."[29] There is the effort to codify the perspectives and behavior patterns of key groups of participants in making foreign policy and national security policy.[30] There is the effort to correlate the expectations of decision-makers in particular cases with the ascertainable consequences of their choices in order to judge the rationality of the action taken.[31] Finally, there has been the rigorous effort by theoretical analysis to break down the decision process into its constituent parts to permit orderly data-collecting by processes that another investigator could reproduce.[32]

In international relations, as in other political sciences, there has been an increasing interest in such theoretical considerations as the

---

[27] *Journal of Conflict Resolution* and the Center for Research on Conflict Resolution.

[28] The Carnegie Endowment for International Peace studies include Stéphane Bernard, *Le conflit franco-marocain, 1943-1956* (Brussels, Editions de l'Institut de sociologie de l'Université libre, 1963, 3 vols.), Jean-Baptiste Duroselle, *Le conflit de Trieste, 1943-1954* (Brussels, Edition de l'Institut de sociologie de l'Université libre, 1967, 3 vols.), and Jacques Freymond, *The Saar Conflict, 1945-1955* (London, Stevens; New York, F. A. Praeger, 1960). Professor Goodrich's monograph is entitled, *Korea: A study of United States Policy in the United Nations* (New York, Council on Foreign Relations, 1956).

[29] See, *e.g.*, Harold Stein, ed., *American Civil-Military Decisions*, University of Alabama Press, 1963.

[30] See Nathan Leites, *A Study of Bolshevism*, Glencoe, Ill., Free Press, 1953. The Institute of War and Peace Studies at Columbia University has commissioned a group of case studies emphasizing civilian and military perspectives in the making of national security policy.

See Warner R. Schilling, Paul Y. Hammond and Glenn H. Snyder, *Strategy, Politics and Defense Budgets*, New York, Columbia University Press, 1962; and Glenn H. Snyder, *Stockpiling Strategic Materials*, San Francisco, Chandler, 1966.

[31] *E.g.*, Bernard C. Cohen, *The Political Process and Foreign Policy*, Princeton, N. J., Princeton University Press, 1957.

[32] *E.g.*, Richard C. Snyder, H. W. Bruck, and Burton M. Sapin, *Decision-making as an Approach to the Study of International Relations*, Princeton, N. J., Foreign Policy Analysis Project, 1954.

choice of the significant questions to be investigated, the clarification of the ordering and integrating concepts in the study, and the construction of abstract models. The "system" in David Easton's *The Political System*[33] and the "process" in David Truman's *The Governmental Process*[34] find an echo in the title of the abstract book by Morton Kaplan, *System and Process in International Politics*.[35] The most ambitious integrating effort has been Quincy Wright's *Study of International Relations*. Kenneth Waltz has recently performed a useful service in inventorying, classifying, and analyzing the resources of classical Western political philosophy for comprehending and coping with the phenomenon of war.[36] His analysis is a salutary reminder for at least a few of today's scholars that it is a voyage of rediscovery on which they are frequently engaged. The Waltz study is, however, exceptional. Most scholars in the last decade with an interest in various theoretical aspects of international relations have not explicitly built on the foundations Waltz describes.[37] It would be more accurate to say that they have been making large excavations on the various sites on which they plan shortly to put in new foundations and hope ultimately to erect large structures.

The fifteen years since the end of World War II have seen a more systematic use of sociology, social psychology, demography, anthropology, and histories of diplomatic and military affairs.[38] The interest in tensions and their alleviation, and in conflicts and their resolution, has brought the international relations scholar into contact with the sociologist and social psychologist.[39] So has the interest in psychological strategy and international communications generally.[40] With Africa and Asia moving to the center of the scholar's

---

[33] New York, Alfred A. Knopf, 1953.

[34] New York, Alfred A. Knopf, 1951.

[35] New York, John Wiley, 1957.

[36] *Man, the State, and War*, New York, Columbia University Press, 1959.

[37] Cf. "Symposium on the Place of Theory in the Conduct and Study of International Relations," Ann Arbor, Mich., University of Michigan, May 12-14, 1960 (mimeographed).

[38] Cf. Alfred Vagts, *Defense and Diplomacy*, New York, King's Crown Press, 1956; and A. F. K. and Katherine Organski, *Population and World Power*, New York, Alfred A. Knopf. Published in 1961.

[39] See Otto Klineberg, *Tensions Affecting International Understanding*, New York, Social Science Research Council, 1950; and Hadley Cantril, ed., *Tensions That Cause War*, Urbana, Ill., University of Illinois Press, 1951.

[40] See the Hoover Institute Studies by Harold D. Lasswell, Daniel Lerner, Ithiel de Sola Pool, and others, bearing the common title, *Revolution and the Development of International Relations*, Stanford, Calif., Stanford University Press, 1951-1952; and Harold D. Lasswell, "Communications as an Emerging Discipline," *Audio-Visual Communication Review*, vi, No. 4 (Fall 1958), pp. 245-54.

attention, the work of the anthropologist has had a new meaning for the student of international relations. The international relations scholar and the historian of diplomacy and military policy have been brought closer together, for the latter has always been studying national policies.[41] Because of his command of the documentary sources and his acceptance of the prevailing multiple-sovereignty system as the natural order, the historian brings to the study of international relations a kind of spontaneous and practical realism which he has not felt needed any grounding in an elaborate theoretical foundation.

Students of international politics, international organization, and international law are being drawn together by their converging efforts to develop their respective specialties as intellectual tools for implementing widely shared values and clarifying choices to be made in national policy.[42] None of these specialists now regards his particular sub-field as an end in itself or as a wholly autonomous specialty. Percy Corbett's *Law in Diplomacy*[43] and the long section in Inis Claude's *Swords into Plowshares*[44] entitled "Approaches to Peace Through International Organization" are examples of this unifying approach oriented to basic values and their realization through the rational selection of national policies.

The Yale Institute of International Studies, beginning in 1943, pioneered in sponsoring a memorandum series addressed to policy-makers and others influential in foreign affairs. Its successor organization after 1951, the Center of International Studies at Princeton University, has contined the practice. In recent years, Congress, and especially the Senate Foreign Relations Committee, has called for reports on broad aspects of policy from academic experts.[45] These reports are widely distributed and promptly reach university students as well as the legislators who are the official consumers of

[41] Two indispensable volumes for the study of World War II are those dealing with United States foreign policy in 1937-1941 by William L. Langer and S. Everett Gleason, *The Challenge to Isolation* and *The Undeclared War* (New York, Harper, 1952 and 1953).

[42] The studies of Harold D. Lasswell and Myres S. McDougal are examples of effective collaboration between a political scientist and a lawyer. See, *e. g.*, McDougal and Lasswell, "The Identification and Appraisal of Diverse Systems of Public Order," *American Journal of International Law,* LIII, No. 1 (January 1959), pp. 1-29.

[43] Princeton, N. J., Princeton University Press, 1959.

[44] New York, Random House, 1956.

[45] *Eg.*, the sixteen studies on *United States Foreign Policy* prepared by different research institutions for the United States Senate, Committee on Foreign Relations, 86th Congress, 1st and 2nd Sessions, Washingon, D.C., G.P.O., 1959-60.

the product. The enhanced prestige of the social scientist today seems to have made his advice more welcome, and his war and postwar experience in government may have developed his taste for prescribing for national policy and strengthened the tendency to concentrate on policy-relevant research.

II

Let us now turn from a consideration of the forces that have been reshaping the American study of international relations to a description of the subject as now taught. Perhaps even more than in political science generally, self-scrutiny has continuously characterized American scholarship in international relations.[46] The survey by Grayson Kirk was the first book-length survey in the postwar period and that by Richard Swift the most recent.[47] The changes in research interest noted in the first section of the latter find their counterpart, though usually only after an interval, in the teaching materials for general courses offered in international relations. National security policy, regional organizations, and international relations theory are all being given increasing attention.

Of the 750 or more accredited American universities and colleges, about 300 have separate departments of political science or of international relations. Only these institutions are likely to offer international relations courses. John Gange estimates that nearly all the significant international relations research comes from forty or fifty of them.[48] This is only a little larger than the number offering the Ph.D. degree in either political science or international relations.

[46] For surveys of political science generally, in addition to Waldo, *op. cit.*, see *Goals for Political Science* (New York, William Sloan Associates, 1951), a report of the Committee for the Advancement of Teaching of the American Political Science Association; also Charles S. Hyneman, *The Study of Politics* (Urbana, Ill., University of Illinois Press, 1959), and Roland Young, ed., *Approaches to the Study of Politics* (Evanston, Ill., Northwestern University Press, 1958), two analyses growing out of a detailed examination of the political science curriculum at Northwestern University. The essay by Heinz Eulau in Bert F. Hoselitz, ed., *A Reader's Guide to the Social Sciences* (Chicago, Ill., University of Chicago Press, 1959), contains many suggestive comments.

[47] Grayson Kirk, *The Study of International Relations in American Colleges and Universities*, New York, Council on Foreign Relations, 1947; and Richard N. Swift, *World Affairs and the College Curriculum,* Washington, D. C., American Council on Education, 1959. The latter is the culminating volume in a series sponsored by the Carnegie Endowment for International Peace which examines various aspects of the study of "world affairs" in American colleges and universities.

[48] John Gange, *University Research on International Affairs,* Washington, D. C., American Council on Education, 1958, p. 12.

For most of the rest, the scope of the international relations courses is largely dictated by the content of the available general textbooks.

The content of the subject, especially in undergraduate courses, is sharply affected by the goals of the teacher. Although training for citizenship is probably as much of a goal in undergraduate international relations teaching as in the teaching of American government, few professors today see their function as the preaching of salvation via the adoption of some particular grand design for world organization or for American foreign policy. Converting the unwashed isolationist masses to the secular religion of internationalism is not the dominant teaching goal of the international relations scholar. His public service motivation and his voluntaristic predispositions do, however, affect his selection of topics for teaching and research.

Whether because the subject is new or because the world is changing so rapidly, there are few acknowledged classics which every serious American student of international relations will be expected to have read; there are as yet no Paretos or Durkheims, no Marshalls or Keyneses, no Bagehots or Diceys. With no core of acknowledged classics and no system of central examinations, each teacher is free to choose his own approach to a general course in international relations. The large number of introductory textbooks is perhaps one indication of the dissatisfaction which most of their writers have felt with the books written prior to their own. Even the size of the American market cannot by itself account for the continuing production of such books and of collections of annotated readings to supplement or to substitute for them.

Several attempts have been made to classify approaches to international relations teaching and research. In Vernon Van Dyke's 1956 summer seminar on the teaching of international politics, four approaches to the study were identified: the institutional, the historical, the philosophical, and the behavioral.[49] It is noteworthy that the social scientists cited to illustrate these four approaches were as often outside the field of international relations as inside. Heterogeneity of approach is apparently characteristic not just of international relations but of the whole of American social science.

Arnold Wolfers has distinguished the "states as actors," "minds of men," and "corporate actors" approaches.[50] The first takes the

---

[49] Vernon Van Dyke, ed., *Some Approaches and Concepts Used in the Teaching of International Politics,* Iowa City, State University of Iowa, 1957.

[50] Arnold Wolfers, "The Actors in International Politics," in William T. R. Fox, ed., *Theoretical Aspects of International Relations,* Notre Dame, Ind., University of Notre Dame Press, 1959, pp. 83-106.

nationstates as given and concentrates on the multiple-sovereignty system as an interaction system;[51] it finds the richest materials for study in diplomatic history. The second stresses the unity of intranational and world politics and makes more use of sociology and social psychology.[52] The third puts "government" rather than "politics" at the center of the study and gives more emphasis to international organization.[53] There are no pure examples of any one of these three approaches at the general textbook level, but the books do differ significantly in their relative emphases.

Still another way of characterizing approaches to the study of international relations is to distinguish the "principles," the "country-by-country," and the "transformations" approaches. Most of the general textbooks exemplify the "principles" approach, although those with a strong historical or geographical emphasis[54] illustrate the second. The experiment at San Francisco State College has emphasized the third, as does the recent text by A. F. K. Organski.[55] These three approaches are complementary rather than incompatible, but the study of such "transformations" as are being wrought by bipolarity, atomic age technology, and the rise of the Afro-Asian nations will receive increasing attention.[56]

Practical limits in approach are set by the gaps in the students' previous historical or social science training.[57] Sometimes this leads

---

[51] *E.g.,* Morgenthau, *Politics Among Nations.*

[52] *E.g.,* Harold D. Lasswell, *World Politics and Personal Insecurity,* New York, McGraw-Hill, 1935; and Frederick S. Dunn, *War and the Minds of Men,* New York, Council on Foreign Relations, 1951.

[53] *E.g.,* Clyde Eagleton, *International Government,* 3rd ed., New York, Ronald Press, 1957.

[54] A recent example is Lennox A. Mills and Charles H. N. McLaughlin, *World Politics in Transition* (New York, Henry Holt, 1956), in which about half the text is devoted to the foreign policies of particular states; an influential earlier work is Harold and Margaret Sprout, eds., *Foundations of National Power* (2nd ed., New York, Van Nostrand, 1951).

[55] See "San Francisco International Studies Project" and "International Studies," San Francisco State College, 1959 and 1960 (mimeographed); and A. F. K. Organski, *World Politics,* New York, Alfred A. Knopf, 1958.

[56] Among the major transformations, that brought about by scientific and technological change has perhaps been least systematically analyzed. The short-run impact on military policy and strategic theory has been widely discussed, but non-military and long-run aspects have been generally neglected in both teaching and research. A few exceptions are John Herz, *International Politics in the Atomic Age,* New York, Columbia University Press, 1959; Philip C. Jessup and Howard Taubenfeld, *Controls for Outer Space and the Antarctic Analogy,* New York, Columbia University Press, 1959; "Science and World Politics" (a symposium), *Journal of International Affairs,* XIII, No. 1 (1959); and John G. Stoessinger, "Atoms for Peace: The International Atomic Energy Agency," in Commission to Study the Organization of Peace, *Organizing Peace in the Nuclear Age,* New York, New York University Press, 1959, pp. 117-233.

[57] Cf. Kirk, *op. cit.,* p. 34: "All social studies are so interrelated that each can best be studied if the beginning student has already studied all the others."

the teacher to "do-it-yourself" efforts to be his own historian,[58] his own student of comparative politics, his own sociologist,[59] his own geographer,[60] his own demographer,[61] his own political philosopher,[62] etc. Extensive digressions to make up for the students' presumed deficiencies make it difficult in many cases to discover the integrating approach and sometimes create doubt that the unexplicated approach is even implicit.[63] Texts with a sustained point of view and closely reasoned argument are likely to be addressed to and most suitable for students who begin their study of international relations at a more advanced stage in their educational careers and who have the factual and intellectual resources to evaluate the argument.

There are many subjects which appear in almost all the treatises and course syllabi we have examined, whatever the basic approach of the particular scholar. Grayson Kirk in 1947 identified "five ingredients" which appeared in almost all the treatises and syllabi: (1) the nature and operation of the state system; (2) basic power factors; (3) the special position and policies of the first-ranking powers; (4) the history of international relations since World War I; and (5) the building of a better world order.[64] Richard N. Swift has summarized the changes since 1947 in the following terms: "Courses today stress power and the complexity of world affairs rather than the state system: they probe deeper into the elements of national power, and in so doing take account of the theoretical and practical results of research in economics, psychology, and sociology. In debating the position of the realists and idealists and presenting the cold war, instructors now pay more attention to theoretical presuppositions; and in presenting accurately the picture of world politics today, they have had to give a larger place than

---

[58] Frederick L. Schuman, *International Politics* (New York, McGraw-Hill, 1st ed., 1933; 6th ed., 1960), is distinctive for its long historical introduction.

[59] Ernst B. Haas and Allen S. Whiting, *Dynamics of International Relations* (New York, McGraw-Hill, 1956), draws on both comparative politics and sociology.

[60] H. and M. Sprout, eds., *op. cit.*

[61] Robert Strausz-Hupé and Stefan T. Possony, *International Relations*, 2nd ed., New York, McGraw-Hill, 1954; and Organski, *World Politics*, *op. cit.*

[62] Hans J. Morgenthau, *Politics Among Nations*, 3rd ed., New York, Alfred A. Knopf, 1960.

[63] Fred A. Sondermann, in "The Study of International Relations: 1956 Version" (*World Politics*, X, No. 1, October 1957, pp. 102-11), distinguishes the texts with a unified conceptual framework from those "strung together . . . in a more or less random fashion." The latter group often contains more factual data than the former.

[64] Kirk, *op. cit.*, pp. 27-29.

ever before to Africa and Asia."[65] Evidently, fashions in teaching have followed the fashions in research described earlier, but usually only after an interval.

In a student's field of undergraduate concentration, courses in international politics, law, and organization are commonly offered. In the more advanced work in the major, students may pursue a variety of courses in non-domestic aspects of economics, law, geography, and possibly other social sciences, and study European and American diplomatic history.

Beyond that, the student often takes special courses in the problems of non-European areas. So little even yet, however, is taught about the non-European world that it is difficult to fill the gaps in knowledge of the history, culture, economy, and politics of various parts of Asia and Africa to the point at which serious analysis becomes possible.[66] Acquiring expertness in any one area is so great a task that it is unusual for a student to be required to do special work in more than one of the areas of non-European culture.

A variety of teaching devices are used to bind together and apply some of the kinds of knowledge that the student has acquired from these varying combinations of courses in international relations, cognate subjects, and area studies. In one sense the course in American foreign policy, which ordinarily deals both with the conduct of American foreign relations and with the analysis of alternative American foreign policies, represents an effort to apply the knowledge previously acquired in courses presented from a "world" point of view. The student looks at the world as seen from Washington, at the situation in which the makers of American foreign policy find themselves, and at the choices which they have to make. Other teaching techniques also have this objective. For example, there are the recent experiments with political gaming as a teaching device in which the students play roles as representatives of various countries negotiating with each other under specified circumstances and do the research to enable them to play these roles.[67]

---

[65] Swift, *op. cit.*, pp. 118-19.

[66] Enthusiasm for area studies sometimes goes so far that the task of filling in the gaps of knowledge about unfamiliar parts of the world may be mistaken for the whole study of international relations. This results from a genuine confusion between "foreign" and "international." If "international" were synonymous with "everything foreign," then one would only have to add up his knowledge of individual areas and call the sum total "international relations."

[67] See Lincoln P. Bloomfield and Norman J. Padelford, "Three Experiments in Political Gaming," *American Political Science Review*, LIII, No. 4 (December, 1959), pp. 105-15; and Herbert Goldhamer and Hans Speier, "Some Observations on Political Gaming," *World Politics*, XII, No. 1 (October, 1959), pp. 71-83.

Another and more widely used method to promote a vicarious sense of participation is the staging of mock political meetings of various kinds. For example, a mock United Nations General Assembly or a mock disarmament commission or a mock Congressional committee hearing is held in which each student or group of students purports to represent a different country or a different point of view.

Only a relatively small proportion of American students are able to travel abroad and, of these, few in any way that is very helpful to their academic study of international relations. Only a small proportion have the opportunity even to visit Washington. Five institutions, with a grant from the Carnegie Corporation—Colgate, Columbia, Princeton, Rutgers, and Swarthmore—have developed a program to send undergraduate honors students to Europe for independent summer research. The results will be carefully watched for the light they throw on a difficult teaching problem.[68]

At the postgraduate level there are two kinds of programs of study in international relations.[69] One is the program which leads toward the Ph.D. degree and university teaching and research. The other is a quasi-professional program which leads toward a master's degree and employment in government or such private fields of international affairs as journalism, finance, or trade. The former program culminates in the writing of a dissertation to test the student's independent research abilities. The latter is likely to have a curriculum which is interdisciplinary and largely prescribed and calls for no comparable experience in independent research.[70]

---

[68] The difficulty of teaching undergraduate students with no foreign travel experience, no direct observation of politics in the national capital, and no simulated international relations experiences in mock meetings and political gaming may be lessened by the rise in standards of television news reporting on world affairs. Documentary presentations on such topics as "The Population Explosion" or "The Munich Crisis" and the showing in full of Nikita Khrushchev's two-hour press conference on the occasion of the abortive summit conference of May, 1960, are examples. Harlan Cleveland, "The Real International World and the Academic Lag," in Roy A. Price, ed., *New Viewpoints in the Social Sciences* (28th Yearbook, Washington, D. C., National Council for the Social Studies, 1958, pp. 172-88), emphasizes the importance of immersion in some foreign culture as a "necessary modern supplement" to the education of every American, not just the student with a specialized concern in the field of International relations.

[69] Cf. C. Dale Fuller, *Training of Specialists in International Relations,* Washington, D. C., American Council on Education, 1957.

[70] It is possible to earn a Ph.D. specializing in international relations and an M.A. as a way-station on the road to the Ph.D. in most of the leading universities, whether in political science or under a separately organized international relations program. The University of Chicago and Yale University were among the first to develop a separately organized Ph.D. program in international relations. The quasi-professional terminal master's degree is offered in

The two types of postgraduate training are not so separate that there are no "cross-over" points. A substantial fraction of the "terminal" master's degree candidates develop a deeper scholarly interest and become candidates for the Ph.D. degree. On the other hand, many of the Ph.D's find careers in government; this appears to be especially true of those with scarce skills in foreign area studies and those with intensive training in economic aspects of international relations.

The traditional three-year period for earning the Ph.D. degree has not ordinarily proved long enough. For the international relations student, all kinds of social science disciplines seem to have tantalizing relevance. More often than not, at least a fourth postgraduate year is required. For the student who is simultaneously pursuing a second program of specialized studies in the problems of some Asian or African or Russian area, it seems to be physically impossible to prepare for the general subjects examinations and to complete a dissertation within the allotted three-year period.

There is no apparent correlation between the organization of international studies within a given university and the availability of courses in special aspects of international relations. Probably, the independent department of international relations or the interdepartmental supervising committee offering a Ph.D. in international relations requires fewer supporting graduate courses in comparative government and political theory and more supporting graduate courses in diplomatic history and the other social sciences. In either case, the choice of options in specialized sub-fields is wide. Each of the leading graduate schools is accordingly turning out men and women of widely varying interests.

One practical consideration may have tended to keep the graduate student in international relations anchored in an established department—usually political science. That consideration is the practical necessity of being employable as an instructor in a department of political science. With the American pattern of requiring the beginning instructor to teach some sections of the introductory course and with that course normally "American Government" if his is a political science department, the prudent graduate student has often combined his international relations studies with enough other political science to compete with political scientists for the

---

a smaller number of institutions. There are separately organized programs for training specialists, for example, at American University, Columbia University, Johns Hopkins University, Princeton University, and Tufts University (Fletcher School of Law and Diplomacy).

available academic vacancies. If there should be an increase in the number of independent departments of international relations, prudence may not operate in exactly the same way.

This article does not deal directly with formal university organization as it relates to the optimum development of the study of international relations. It would, however, be a matter of concern if formal organization within the university limited free exchange among professors with related intellectual interests and made it difficult for a student of one of these professors to indulge his curiosity about the intellectual output of all the others.

Many universities have developed special research institutes focusing on international relations. These institutes have had an impact on the growth of the subject disproportionate to the number of scholars involved. Special financing has facilitated more ample staffing to the point at which intellectual "chain reactions" can more easily occur and at which a few post-doctoral fellows and research assistants can have an apprentice relation with senior professors for which formal teaching is no substitute.[71] Membership in an institute creates an obligation to do research and an immediate environment receptive to it, to say nothing of providing the free time to engage in it. The research institute in international studies has the virtue of its vice, a preoccupation with program planning. The vice is distracting concern with discovering a continuing basis for financial support; the virtue is that the periodic necessity for making advance explanations to justify a special allocation of funds involves a self-conscious emphasis on "research design."[72] For international relations research, which often involves the cooperation of scholars from several disciplines, the research institute is of particular importance.

In a less hectic period of less crowded lecture halls, it may have been easier to combine full-time teaching with the research necessary for an international relations scholar to maintain his full intellectual vigor. The drain on professorial energies involved in advising students is very great for the teachers of both undergraduates

[71] Gange (*op. cit.*, pp. 27-28) comments on the decline in the use of the pre-doctoral research assistant and the increase in the number of fellowships for which no service is expected and no special research training is received.

[72] The RAND Corporation is *sui generis*. Although an outstanding example of "operations research" with unmatched government financial support and access for its staff to classified information and to the decision-making levels of government, it has many of the characteristics of an academic research organization. Social scientists on the RAND staff have increasingly been a source of leadership in international relations research. Their contributions to the study of military policy and strategic theory have already been cited, but they are influential in other fields, too.

and graduates in the United States. In the former case, a classroom teaching schedule of twelve or even fifteen hours a week is not uncommon. In the latter case, the burden of supervising an increasing number of doctoral dissertations can be heavy. The proliferation of research institutes, post-doctoral fellowships, travel grants, and *ad hoc* arrangements for financing summer and sabbatical leave research in part offsets the factors which otherwise would make it difficult to combine teaching and research in this field of increasing student popularity.

Discussions about the use of "the case method," "the problem approach," "the decision-making focus," etc., reflect the vitality of the international relations teacher's concern with effective intellectual communication. Some of these discussions, however, have an air of unreality because they imply a prior and largely nonexistent consensus—or, if existing, an infrequently explicated consensus—as to what is to be taught. A case of what? An approach to what category of problems? A focus on what kind of decisions? Individuals have sought to provide explicit answers to these questions,[73] but a consensus as to a preferred teaching method is artificial unless it rests upon a consensus as to the subject to be taught.

These more fundamental questions are not easily answerable except by persons whose sense of conviction as to the significant questions is rooted in perspectives formed as they have made choices regarding their own research. Research grows out of a conviction as to what are significant questions. So does a sustainable point of view about the scope and organizing concepts of such an emerging discipline as international relations. An intellectual climate favorable to research appears to be essential to good teaching.

III

These comments on the teaching of international relations in the United States may be brought into sharper focus by comparing the situations of the American teacher with that of some of his colleagues in Europe and certain parts of the British Commonwealth. The teacher-researcher requires free time in isolation, but he cannot be totally isolated from his fellow scholars of related interests.

In a country of continental size, it is almost as difficult and expensive to come from the West Coast to Washington and New York

[73] *E.g.*, Snyder *et al.*, *op. cit.*

as it is to go from the East Coast to London and Paris. Professional contacts, therefore, have to be planned. In less decentralized countries, the national capital is the focus of intellectual as well as of political life, and the need for *intra*national arrangements for maintaining an academic communications network by formal organization is much less. The United States already has within itself some of the characteristics common to the whole NATO coalition, and indeed also common to the non-NATO countries of Western Europe and to much of the British Commonwealth outside NATO—shared intellectual interests and closely related cultures, but with wide regional variations and great decentralization. It is logical to find emerging within this broader community, on a *trans*national basis, some of the functional equivalents of the associations of professional scholars,[74] the Social Science Research Council,[75] the Carnegie Endowment for International Peace,[76] *ad hoc* conferences to discuss common problems of teaching and research,[77] all of which had to be brought into being to give what coherence there is to the American study of international relations.

In the next decade some of the problems which have emerged in the United States will be seen as problems of the extended North American-West European-British Commonwealth family of scholars in international relations. As this extended family of scholars becomes more closely knit, it too will struggle to find unity in the diversity of its intellectual approaches and teaching methods. Ad-

[74] Although membership in the International Political Science Association is open to scholars throughout the world, active participants come mainly from the North Atlantic community. The Association has probably done much more to strengthen contacts within this regional community than between the North Atlantic group of scholars and those in other parts of the world.

[75] In addition to the Committee on National Security Policy Research already cited, the Social Science Research Council has had a series of committees on the study of various foreign areas and on the comparative politics of underdeveloped areas which have also brought together scholars with international relations interests. Nearly thirty years ago, an SSRC committee under James T. Shotwell called for the creation of an Institute of Atlantic Affairs. The SSRC formerly had a committee on international relations research, out of whose work grew two general analyses—Frederick S. Dunn, "The Present Course of International Relations Research," *World Politics*, II, No. 1 (October, 1949), pp. 80-95; and William T. R. Fox, "Interwar International Relations Research: The American Experience," see pp. 1-13.

[76] The Carnegie Endowment has for many years had an office in Europe as well as its main office in New York. Formerly in Paris, it is now in Geneva.

[77] Participants in the meetings of the International Studies Conference, founded in 1929, have been drawn almost entirely from North Atlantic countries. Thus, except for the Australian chairman, Professor W. R. Crocker, the whole membership of the Windsor meeting on the university teaching of international relations in March, 1950, was from these countries. See Geoffrey L. Goodwin, ed., *The University Teaching of International Relations*, Oxford, Blackwell, 1951.

justing the subject matter to the great transformations in contemporary world politics is a problem for European and Commonwealth as well as American scholars. Increases in numbers of students, such as have engulfed the American teacher of international relations, will pose similar problems in Europe. There will be a call on both sides of the Atlantic for the same searching examination of the value patterns which are the common property of the Western constitutional democracies for their relevance to the definition of the national interest and to a shared definition of interests of the North Atlantic and British Commonwealth nations.[78] The body of social science out of which the study of international relations has sprung is also the common property of the Western scholarly community, and the American interest in ordering data-collecting processes by analysis of fundamental theoretical concepts is in response to a common intellectual impulse.[79]

Meanwhile, the current of ideas will continue to move both ways across the Atlantic Ocean. The universities of America will continue to appoint to their faculties European scholars. The European members of the fraternity of international relations scholars will no doubt continue to be constructively critical of what one of them has described as "too audacious a synthesis,"[80] at least at the present stage of research and analysis. They will continue to question the existence of a distinctive method or focus in the American study of international relations. They may be skeptical of the compatibility of voluntaristic civic zeal and unrestrained scholarly curiosity as motives for developing the subject. They may be impatient with an overconcentration of American scholarly attention upon Soviet-American relations. Some of them may even see this as an effort to endow the bipolar world order with a new legitimacy; they will certainly view it as detracting attention from problems presently capable of constructive solution. Finally, Western Europe vis-à-vis

---

[78] *E.g.,* Eulau, *loc. cit.;* Stanley Hoffmann, "International Relations: The Long Road to Theory," *World Politics,* XI, No. 3 (April, 1959), pp. 346-77; and Hoffmann, ed., *Contemporary Theory in International Relations,* Englewood Cliffs, N. J., Prentice-Hall, 1960.

[79] L. F. Richardson, "Generalized Foreign Politics," *British Journal of Psychology* (Monograph supplement, Vol. XXIII, Cambridge, Eng., 1939), and Maurice A. Ash, "An Analysis of Power, with Special Reference to International Politics" (*World Politics*, III, No. 2, January, 1951, pp. 218-37), are examples of theoretical analyses by English scholars which have aroused the interest of American scholars with comparable theoretical concerns. Richardson's work on the mathematical theory of war was the subject of a symposium issue of the *Journal of Conflict Resolution* (I, No. 3, September, 1957). His posthumous works, *Arms and Insecurity* and *Statistics of Deadly Quarrels* have recently been published (Chicago, Quadrangle Books, 1960).

[80] Grosser, *loc. cit.*, p. 639.

the Soviet Union and the United States is like Northern Italy in the time of the first incursions of the great powers from across the Alps. Like Machiavelli at the end of the fifteenth century, the scholars of Western Europe may bring to their analyses of world politics qualities of perception and objectivity difficult for either Soviet or American scholars to achieve.[81]

There is one direction in which the American study of international relations has not moved and for which there does not yet seem to be much call on either side of the Atlantic. This is the comparative study of multiple-sovereignty systems. After all, the present state system is only one among many which have existed or may exist in the future.[82] If the student of international relations is to fulfill the voluntaristic aspirations suggested in the preceding pages, he must be able to transcend his own time and culture. Only then can he gain understanding as to what aspects of our state system are inherent in any multiple-sovereignty system and what aspects are capable of transformation into a system which will more efficiently implement the values of our free Western society.

---

[81] *Ibid,* p. 651. Professor Grosser also comments on the advantage enjoyed by European scholars in "not belonging to a country which plays such a decisive role in world politics. . . ."

[82] Morton A. Kaplan, in *System and Process in International Politics* (*op. cit.*, chap. 2), identifies six types of international system: the "balance of power" system, the loose bipolar system, the tight bipolar system, the universal system, the hierarchial system, and the unit veto system. He does not claim to be able to cite historical examples of each of the six types.

III

FREDERICK SHERWOOD DUNN AND THE AMERICAN STUDY OF INTERNATIONAL RELATIONS

From *World Politics,* Vol. XV, October, 1962

"The great difference between foreign affairs in books and foreign affairs in action lies in this, that foreign affairs in action consists largely of doubts and confusion, of difficult choices based on insufficient knowledge and dimly perceived objectives, followed by the same thing all over again, whereas foreign affairs in books commonly appear as definite, orderly, and rational."—From an unpublished manuscript by Frederick S. Dunn, ca. 1942.

As legal officer in the Department of State in the 1920's, Frederick S. Dunn developed a curiosity about the decision-making process of which he was a part. The dissatisfaction which he felt with prevailing explanations of state behavior, and particularly with single-factor explanations, was the spur to a lifetime of scholarly activity.[1]

[1] Frederick Sherwood Dunn (1893-1962) was born in New York City. He graduated from Princeton University in 1914 and took a law degree at New York University in 1917. He served in France in World War I in the A.E.F. as First Lieutenant in the Tank Corps. In the 1920's he was Assistant Solicitor in the Department of State. He was associate counsel in the American and British Claims Arbitration and attorney for the United States Agency in the Mixed Claims Commission, United States and Mexico. Professor Dunn took his Ph.D. degree at Johns Hopkins in 1928 and was from 1930 to 1935 executive secretary of the Walter Hines Page School of International Relations at Johns Hopkins and Creswell Lecturer in International Law at the same institution. In 1935 he became Professor of International Relations at Yale and from 1940 to

His quest for greater knowledge relevant to the ordering and control of foreign affairs was to lead him successively to Johns Hopkins, Yale, and Princeton Universities and far afield from the methods and subjects of interest to his colleagues in international law; but there was a forty-year continuity of interest in a set of questions whose answers would lead to improved decision-making.[2]

Participation in the work of two international claims commissions had convinced him that legal considerations alone could neither account for nor provide the basis for predicting what would happen to a given claim. At Johns Hopkins University, Walter Wheeler Cook and his colleagues were finding a new understanding of municipal law and the legal process in their sociological jurisprudence. Frederick S. Dunn blazed the way for a similar development in international law in three monographic studies and several journal articles.[3]

He wrote that "The conventional idea of the legal process rests upon the assumption that it is possible to develop a body of rules and standards of conduct which will, if properly applied, normally yield one and only one answer to each new problem falling within its scope. It appears in fact that, in doubtful or novel cases, the existing body of rules and principles generously provides, not one, but two or more precepts logically applicable to the question at issue, each one leading to a different answer. How the selection is made between these competing precepts is the crucial point in every case, yet, under the prevailing view of the nature of the legal process, the method by which this selection is made remains a mystery."[4]

Throughout his career, Mr. Dunn also gave short shrift to other types of simplification, but particularly to those that suggest that evil or materialistic men have somehow come to occupy the key

---

1951 was in addition Director of the Yale Institute of International Studies. Princeton University awarded him an L.L.D. degree *honoris causa* in 1949, and in 1951 invited him to return as Albert G. Milbank Professor of International Law and Practice and as Director of its new Center of International Studies. He retired in 1961 and during 1961-1962 taught a course in international relations at Bryn Mawr College.

[2] See, for example, his introduction to *Peace-making and the Settlement with Japan*, (posthumously published, Princeton University Press, 1963) in which there is a self-contained essay on the dilemmas and perplexities of the decision-maker in foreign affairs (pp. xii-xviii).

[3] *The Practice and Procedure of International Conferences* (Baltimore, 1928); *The Protection of Nationals* (Baltimore, 1932); and *The Diplomatic Protection of Americans in Mexico* (New York, 1933). See also the journal articles cited below for the 1927-1930 period.

[4] *Protection of Nationals*, 10.

points of decision-making and have only to be turned out. He was severe in his judgment of Sumner Welles' *Where Are We Heading?* He knew Welles to be experienced and intelligent and obviously felt Welles' readers deserved better. In his words, ". . . what Mr. Welles has done is to fall into the ancient error of seeing a devil behind everything that is unsatisfactory in our relations with the rest of the world. His method of analysis is based on the implied assumption that if anything is amiss in our foreign affairs, it must be due to some stupidity or lack of knowledge or downright venality of some particular official. . . . The means of practical improvement in foreign affairs lie not so much in finding people to blame for what is unsatisfactory as in discovering new ways of mutual accommodation between the conflicting interests and viewpoints of independent states." [5]

Similarly, while paying due respect to John U. Nef for the historical scholarship in *War and Human Progress*,[6] he judged Nef also to have neglected to mobilize the relevant social science findings by which he might have tested his belief that man had only to curb his passions to exorcise the evil spirit of war and bring peace.

> As a matter of fact, the Communist leaders have shown little concern over their comforts, their lusts or even over their lives. Their motivations cannot be explained in simple terms of human corruption or in the traditional categories of common sense. It is a false diagnosis which suggests that such people can be redeemed and made more pacific by being encouraged to exercise more freely the human faculties of love, craftsmanship and grace.
> Professor Nef gives little attention to the recent advances that have been made in the understanding of group behavior and the ways of influencing men's attitudes.[7]

Welles, the diplomatist, and Nef, the economic historian, had in their post-World War II writing, in Frederick S. Dunn's eyes, exhibited the kind of intellectual vice which he thought he had found in the lawyers of the post-World War I period. Whitehead, in his view, had described it very well: "The man with a method good for purposes of his dominant interests, is a pathological case in respect to his wider judgment on the coordination of this method with a more complete experience. . . . We all start by being em-

[5] "Mr. Welles Dissents," *Yale Review*, xxxvi (Winter 1947), 343-344.
[6] Cambridge, Mass., 1950.
[7] *Political Science Quarterly*, LXVI (June, 1951), 303.

piricists. But our empiricism is confined within our immediate interests. The more clearly we grasp the intellectual analysis of a way regulating procedure for the sake of those interests, the more decidedly we reject the inclusion of evidence which refuses to be immediately harmonized with the method before us. Some of the major disasters of mankind have been produced by the narrowness of men with a good methodology." [8]

It was, however, the inadequacy of conventional modes of legal analysis *to answer the particular questions he was asking* to which, down to the mid-1930's, Professor Dunn addressed himself. Note that he never asserted the inappropriateness of the conventional analysis for the intellectual operation for which it was originally developed. He only denied that it helped him order, explain, predict, or control what went on in Foreign Offices. He did not, for example, find convincing an analysis of successor-state obligations which cited John Quincy Adams' statement of 1823 affirming Colombia's legal obligations as the successor state to Spain. Dunn knew that United States officials had earlier been as eager to divest themselves of successor-state obligations following the American Revolution as were Colombian officials following Colombia's war of independence. "The law," he thought, could not account for both the earlier and the later American position.[9]

What then were the "unacknowledged factors that influence legal decisions"? [10] It would have been easy enough to say "self-interest"; but this slurred over for Professor Dunn the really interesting questions as to what selves happened to have what interests promoted and maintained by Foreign Office activity, and how an identifiable set of officials came to perceive those selves and those interests as the ones to be served. It also slurred over the even more interesting questions as to how these officials would have perceived those selves and those interests with greater and better-organized knowledge of the world environment in which they were acting and greater awareness of their own roles in serving those interests. Evidently, conventional ideas of self-interest provided no more of a basis than conventional ideas of law for developing rules and standards which, if properly applied, would normally yield one and only one answer to a problem falling within their scope.

[8] A. N. Whitehead, *The Function of Reason* (1929), quoted in Dunn, *Protection of Nationals*, 4.

[9] "The New International Status of the British Dominions," *Virginia Law Review*, XIII (March, 1927), 376-77.

[10] This is the title of Chapter 6 of *Protection of Nationals*.

Although not a utopian, Dunn was a meliorist who believed that with greater knowledge and self-awareness Foreign Office officials would more often make choices which would have the consequences they expected and desired.

Writing before Adolf Hitler had shattered the Versailles order, Dunn could say:

> Wars and alliances and balances of power have the appeal of grandeur, and are the traditional preoccupation of diplomatists and of students of international relations. But the average foreign office official or diplomatist discovers, often to his surprise and pain, that there is given him little opportunity to exercise his mind and skill upon them. The subject-matter of his daily note-writing and his conferences is apt to be concerned primarily with the safeguarding of the interests of his fellow-citizens in their activities that extend beyond the borders of their own country.
>
> This is, of course, especially true of the United States. Owing to its isolated geographical position and its relative size, its officials are relieved of the necessity of thinking continuously about maintaining its security from attack by its neighbors. Its contacts with other nations originate primarily in the commercial and social activities of its citizens abroad, and, to a lesser extent, in the activities of citizens of other nations within its own territories. Its paramount interests in the field of international relations seem to be grouped around the preservation and advancement of these foreign activities of its citizens.[11]

This may seem to be a parochial viewpoint, considering the dramatic involvement of the United States in the high politics of the world less than ten years after he wrote. It was, however, an accurate description of what the officials were actually doing—or could have been doing, given the temper of American traditions and American public opinion regarding European involvements. For anyone with Professor Dunn's intellectual interests in improved policy-making, the contemporary literature on international relations which described and evaluated steps in American foreign policy in terms of progress toward or away from international government was largely irrelevant.

Frederick S. Dunn saw that legal concepts and precepts appropriate to interstate relations in the pre-Industrial Revolution world of relatively isolated communities where economic and social life were localized had to be modified to meet the needs for orderly intercourse of men whose persons, goods, funds, and ideas were in

[11] *Ibid.*, 12-13.

ever-increasing amounts crossing state boundaries.[12] Inevitably, legal norms were shaped by the dominant ideas of capitalist Europe, the home of the great states of the Western state system.

Thus, diplomatic protection could best be understood as a substitute for territorial conquest. It was a practice which harmonized the interests in trade and investment of the nationals of the great states and of the Europeanized part of the world with the interests of nationals of the lesser and non-European states in avoiding the extinction of their countries' sovereignty.[13] Nor did he doubt that the practice of diplomatic protection would be greatly changed if the non-European and non-capitalist states gained in power.

The first "unacknowledged factor" in the behavior of Foreign Office officials was then their failure to see as relative the standards of justice and reason which they asserted as absolutely binding on governments with whom some conflict had arisen. These standards were derived, Dunn concluded, from largely unexamined assumptions about the prevailing world order and the place of the official's own country in it. He proposed to help the decision-maker master the sources of his own irrationality by exposing the role which intuition, prejudice, outworn postulates, doctrinaire methods, and hidden ethical concepts were actually playing.[14] Ideological blinders derived from stereotypes associated with nationality, class, and profession would be removed.

There were other unacknowledged factors more specifically associated with the holding of official position. In this "public office" category, Dunn included the distortions and irrationalities, induced by the need to have some decision which one can subsequently justify and the consequent temptation to cite and to follow a convenient precedent without inquiring too closely as to its suitability. He also showed how the tyranny of administrative habit and, in legal decisions at least, the desire to maintain the respect of the members of one's own profession could keep methods of choice

---

[12] *Ibid.*, 28ff. Professor Dunn had earlier written that ". . . if we examine the cases in which the responsibility of states for injuries to aliens within their borders has been successfully invoked, we find that this minimum standard of justice is nothing more or less than the ideas which are conceived to be essential to a continuation of the existing social and economic order of European capitalistic civilization. . . . And so long as these states remain dominant in the international society, it is the fundamentals of their civilization which will determine the content of the standard of justice embodied in the international legal system."—"International Law and Private Property Rights," *Columbia Law Review*, XXVIII (February, 1928), 175-76.

[13] *Protection of Nationals*, 355-58.

[14] *Ibid.*, 85.

running in accustomed grooves, whether or not the conditions that originally accounted for those methods still obtained. He noted the operation, where the available precepts afforded some latitude of choice, of a "prophylactic factor" (what decision will discourage the recurrence of this deviation from the norm of desired behavior?) and a "revenge factor" (what does the affected party "deserve"?). His wish was not that these last considerations should never operate, but that they should operate only when they were explicitly recognized and the consequences candidly examined.[15]

If there seemed to Dunn as a pioneer in the new sociological international jurisprudence a discrepancy between the "real" unacknowledged factors governing an official's behavior and the "right" legal arguments adduced in support of that behavior, he was careful not to impute bad faith to men whom he saw as merely confused. Thus, he rejected the scandal variant of imperalist explanations for state behavior. He concluded that ". . . the popular imperialist interpretation . . . assumes a singleness of purpose and an unfailing ingenuity in working toward it, which, to anyone familiar with the hesitant and uncertain actions of foreign offices at first hand, must seem in most cases a fantastic illusion. It implies at the same time that otherwise apparently intelligent and high-minded individuals invariably lose a large proportion of these qualities when endowed with the responsibilities of public office in the handling of foreign affairs." [16]

Perhaps the major deception which the decision-maker habitually practiced was self-deception; he often believed he was solving a technical problem when he was in fact making a political choice. He had the persisting fantasy that with more facts about the particular case he was scrutinizing, his doubts and confusion would go away, but his perplexities really grew from his reluctance to recognize that he was making a choice.[17] Professor Dunn's viewpoint was that, with a better mobilization of the potential contributions of social science, the consequences of a given official action would more often correspond to the expectations of the decision-maker at the moment of choice. When he used phrases like "better choices" or "improved decision-making," there was no element of normative ambiguity; the test was the degree of correlation between expectations and consequences.

---

[15] *Ibid.*, Chapter 6.
[16] *Ibid.*, 24.
[17] *Peace-making and the Settlement with Japan,* Introduction.

If research was to lead to improved public policy, it should concentrate on exposing inappropriate existing techniques of analysis. As Dunn wrote in connection with his Mexican study: "It is unfortunate that in spite of the great advances made in recent years in scientific method and in our knowledge of the intellectual processes, the science of international law still rests upon such ambiguous terms as 'justice' and 'reason.' Many writers apparently assume that it is possible to deduce automatically by the simple laws of logic concrete answers to specific problems from general propositions containing such variable terms. . . . It is of little help to us in attempting to solve the Mexican problem to say that nations are bound to observe a minimum standard of justice in their treatment of foreigners, unless we know what goes on in the minds of the societal agents charged with the settlement of the dispute when they seek to apply this criterion of judgment. To discover this we need only look at the specific acts which have actually been considered in the past as in violation of this standard of justice by nations in their dealings with each other."[18]

Only thus could international law be seen for what it was, an institution responsive to society's need to cope with all "the difficulties and clashes of interest arising out of the tremendous flow of peoples and goods across the border of nations."[19] Regarding the need and the institution responsive to that need, Professor Dunn wrote: "The continuance of our daily social and economic activities along their accustomed plane has become dependent upon keeping open the channels of intercourse and trade throughout the whole of the world. This in turn depends upon *the maintenance of some sort of definite orderly arrangement* of this intercourse so that the activities of others may be permanently counted upon to assure regularity of action and far-reaching scope of plans. Arrangements of this sort are ordinarily the work of organized political institutions, yet the absence of any such institution for the world as a unit has not prevented the formulation of a body of rules to keep up with the enlarging economic activities of man. These rules make up what we know as international law, which may be described as the collection of habits and precepts of conduct which have grown up out of *the need for bringing about security and predictability in the social and economic intercourse across political borders.* These rules are not only related to the international social and economic

[18] "International Law and Private Property Rights," 175.
[19] *Ibid.*, 170.

order; they are the verbal symbols of that order. And like all systems of law based primarily on custom, they make no provision for revolutionary changes in that order." [20]

In his first published law review article, dealing with the international legal status of the British Dominions following the Imperial Conference of 1926, he boldly proclaimed the necessity to look outside "rigid legal forms" to find applicable law: "To know the real status of the Dominions at the present time, it is not enough to look at the constitutional form of the Empire. Legal forms are rigid and tend to remain in existence long after the conditions which gave them birth have passed away. If we look at the real operation of the Imperial system as it has developed in recent years we find a wholly different situation both within the Empire and without." [21] Nor did he find any more helpful the corpus of international law, with its oversupply of mutually incompatible and frequently inexact precedents regarding the rights and duties of successor states.

In his detailed studies of the diplomatic protection of Americans in Mexico, he found evaluations of the legality of Mexican confiscations as little helpful as he had the legal literature on state succession when he dealt with the new status of the British Dominions. He exhibited a remarkable precocity in anticipating the consequences for international law of what a generation later was called the "revolution of rising expectations." Regarding the claims of Americans which grew out of land reforms in the homeland of the twentieth century's first semi-colonial revolution, he wrote: "Most of the current discussion of the controversy has turned about the question of whether the legislative acts of the Mexican Government really were 'confiscatory,' and whether or not the titles of the former owners were valid under Mexican laws. But these questions, important as they are, do not touch upon the main issue. The fact of the matter is that the Mexican revolutionary government *had* to take the land away from the existing owners and give it to the natives, however 'legal' may have been the titles of the existing owners. That government is not now in a position to retrace its steps, nor is it able to make adequate monetary retribution to the owners whose lands have been and are being taken away. Accordingly, from the standpoint of international law, the question that primarily has to be answered is whether foreign governments have

[20] *Ibid.*, 170-71 (italics added).
[21] "New International Status of the British Dominions," 357.

a right to intervene to bring about the modification of legislation adopted by the government of a country ostensibly to improve social and economic conditions among its citizens but which cannot be carried out without causing substantial losses to foreigners who had duly acquired property interests which were protected under the prior laws of that country."[22] He specifically foresaw that it was necessary for the instrument of diplomatic protection in particular and the institution of international law in general to get out of the way of bona fide social reform.

> To extend the rule of the inviolability of the property rights of aliens to cover all cases of expropriation without concurrent indemnity, regardless of whether such act is deemed to be a necessary step in the improvement of conditions of the native population, would seem to place a powerful obstacle in the way of future social reform.[23]
>
> From a functional point of view, a possible solution would be to retain the rule of intervention but to except from its operation all governmental acts infringing upon vested property rights which were the result of *bona fide* social or economic reform, genuinely aimed to benefit the nation as a whole, and were not discriminatory against foreigners as such, nor liable to disturb to any substantial extent the existing methods of carrying on intercourse between nations.[24]

Perhaps his most often-cited contribution to what Frederick S. Dunn liked to think of as "the rational science" of international law, the science which clarifies the common interests and makes the legal process better serve the practical ends of statesmen, is the principle of risk allocation to which his studies of diplomatic protection led him. He defined this principle as follows: "Where a failure to prosecute is such that, if generalized, it would lead to conditions unfavorable to the customary course of intercommunity relationships, then international responsibility would be engaged."[25] Note that Dunn claimed for his principle of risk allocation no earth-shaking significance. He advanced it modestly and as an illustration of similar rules and standards which could be developed by the same patient investigation of other problems on which international lawyers were called upon to work.

---

[22] "International Law and Private Property Rights," 169-70.
[23] *Ibid.*, 178.
[24] *Ibid.*, 180.
[25] *Protection of Nationals*, 187.

Changed conditions could not be dealt with by unchanged law, and even in the narrow area of Professor Dunn's most intensive research, the diplomatic protection of Americans in Mexico, he never supposed that the risk-allocation principle or any other legal formulation would permanently harmonize the clash of interests. He concluded that "It would be absurd to suppose . . . that the subject of diplomatic protection has been permanently removed as a source of serious controversy between the two countries. A change of administration that should bring the Mexican government into weaker hands, a resurgence of revolutionary activity, a renewed shortage of oil in the United States, a revival of anti-foreign feeling, or any other event that seemed to threaten existing American interests in Mexico, would quickly recreate the conditions that have led to controversy in the past and again put to the test the machinery that has been devised for the peaceful solution of disputes of this character." [26]

If new law to regulate new developments in international daily life was not simply to be deduced from old precepts and old precedents, where was it to be found? The answer was, partly in better decision-making by national officials—i.e., decisions which better harmonized the interests of conflicting parties—but partly also in international legislation. Professor Dunn asserted that "In such a rapidly growing community as the society of nations, it would be inconceivable that we should long remain without some kind of legislative process to bring the law within hailing distance, at least, of the needs of international intercourse. The existence of the postulates of sovereignty and equality might make the development of such a process difficult, but they would not permanently stand in the way of the expanding social interests of the ultimate members of the community. International intercourse does not exist *because* of these postulates, but because men *want* to trade with each other and to travel and reap the fruits of a wider civilization than is possible within the limits of artificial national boundaries." [27]

Although Professor Dunn's interests gradually shifted from international law and organization to diplomacy and politics, particularly after he went to Yale in 1935, his interest never flagged in

[26] *Diplomatic Protection of Americans in Mexico,* 423.

[27] "International Legislation," *Political Science Quarterly,* XLII (December, 1927), 576. In a similar vein, he quotes Brierly on the same page: "Law is still thinking in terms of rights; states are thinking of interests and demanding that they be protected" (*British Yearbook of International Law,* 1924, p. 16).

seeking to discover the ways in which all the institutions of international life could be used to adjust conflict. Where the common interest was manifest, there was no intellectual problem. Where it was not, international institutions were to be judged by their success or failure in harmonizing them; and it was the highest task of the international relations scholar to point the ways toward harmonization. [28]

His book, *The Practice and Procedure of International Conferences* (1928), based on his Johns Hopkins doctoral dissertation, showed the same tendency as his writing on diplomatic protection to look outside the law and to the intentions and interests of the parties for the emerging law. It was the needs of "the new international public" which the law had to serve. Dunn wrote that ". . . two developments which began in the latter part of the eighteenth century and have continued up to the present time have completely changed both the substance of international relations and the methods by which they are conducted. The first of these was the industrial revolution and the second was the rise of popular government. These developments have not only altered the nature and extent of the relations between states as *political entities,* but have also given us an entirely new international public with a new type of international relations which did not exist at the time when the classical theories of international jurisprudence were formulated. This fact is of great importance, for it largely explains why, in a theoretically unorganized collection of independent political entities enjoying exclusive territorial jurisdiction, we find such a surprising number of permanent international agencies engaged in the regulation of transnational interests and activities on a community basis. For if it is true that no government can exist without a public, it is equally true that no public which has become conscious of its common interests remains very long without the establishment

[28] The catholicity of Mr. Dunn's interest in whatever social science would help him in answering his questions is illustrated by the precocious concern he showed in 1928, in his first book, for what would now be called "small-group sociology." Thus, in discussing factors affecting the procedure of international conferences, he wrote: ". . . the mere matter of size is an important factor in determining the course of conference procedure. This is true whether the conference be one of diplomats or of dentists. It is common experience that where a large number of persons confer together for the purpose of reaching a common agreement, certain difficulties of procedure are encountered which are not present in small gatherings. There seems to be, in fact, a definite limit to the size of the group which can carry on an intelligent exchange of views without formal organization. This limit varies somewhat with the character and composition of the conference, but it exists for every deliberative body no matter how homogeneous."— *Practice and Procedure of International Conferences,* 25.

of instruments of government."[29] He developed a useful distinction between the bargaining conference (diplomacy in multilateral form) and the legislative conference (multilateral international contract).[30] It was the latter type primarily which served the "non-political" needs of the new international public.

The growth of the law by multilateral contract among changing combinations of states, as well as by customary rules in particular regimes of the world, reflected Dunn's view that "In reality the interests and activities of the nations of the world, which it is the function of international law to regulate, are practically never co-extensive with the territory of the world community. . . . The society of nations is not, in fact, a homogeneous society. . . . They differ widely in size, in state of civilization and in the nature and scope of their external relations."[31]

In 1935 Mr. Dunn left Johns Hopkins to become Professor of International Relations and a member of the Yale Institute of International Studies, then being established with Nicholas J. Spykman as its first director. At Yale Professor Dunn's unconventional graduate teaching in international law, organization, and diplomacy led him to develop as a field for instruction and Ph.D. examination purposes "methods and instruments of control."[32] This description of a field of special study was his intellectual trade-mark. The deteriorating climate of European and Far Eastern politics, and perhaps also the intellectual stimulation of New Haven as symbolized by Professor Spykman and Arnold Wolfers, had shifted Dunn's interest away from the activities of lawyers in Foreign Offices coping with the problems of "the new international public" toward those of political officials coping with threats to the foundations of the world order. However, he brought to the new problems a viewpoint which had matured in his earlier international legal research.

Peaceful Change, a small book published in 1937, reflected both the sustained viewpoint and the new focus on problems of war and peace.[33] Dunn's concern was still the development of international

[29] *Ibid.*, 10.
[30] *Ibid.*, 40.
[31] "International Legislation," 587.
[32] The Yale University Graduate School Announcement of the Graduate Program in International Relations for 1962-1963 still lists "Methods and Instruments of Control" as one of the five fields of instruction.
[33] *Peaceful Change: A Study of International Procedures* (New York, 1937). This study was also printed as "U. S. Memorandum No. 3" for the Tenth International Studies Conference held in Paris in June and July of 1937. Professor Dunn was the rapporteur of the subcommittee on procedural methods of peaceful change of the Committee of Experts which planned the American

procedures and Foreign Office methods of analysis which would, to the greatest extent possible, harmonize conflicting interests.

It perhaps tells more about the United States than about Professor Dunn that as late as 1937—after the Manchurian and Ethiopian Incidents and after the remilitarization of the Rhineland—so much attention was being paid to preserving peace by developing procedures for peaceful change and so little to preserving it by strengthening the machinery of enforcement. *Peaceful Change* anticipates by two years E. H. Carr's *Twenty Years' Crisis* both in its emphasis on peaceful change and its lack of attention to enforcement.[34] He also anticipated David Mitrany in seeing the problem not as one of getting unwilling states to yield up territory but as one of lessening the extent to which existing boundaries frustrate human activity and thus reduce the pressure for shifting them.[35] Thus, he wrote: "A beginning might be made by the adoption of genuine open-door policies with respect to the exploitation of raw materials everywhere. These policies should be incorporated in international agreements because otherwise they would be subject to frequent change and would instill no confidence in other states. Eventually it might be possible to establish a system of international supervision of the operation of these agreements in order to give assurance that they were being carried out in good faith. But real progress cannot be expected until some means can be found to lessen the feelings of insecurity which now cause nations to subordinate everything to the building up of national power." [36]

Dunn recognized clearly that it was credible threats, not objectively determined needs, which in the 1930's was stimulating "peaceful" change. It was the demands of Nazi Germany, not the needs of Austria, which was likely to bring, short of war, a change in the *status quo*.[37] No special procedures needed to be invented to facilitate such a change. As for the powers unable or unwilling to make credible threats, he found only very modest opportunities

studies for that conference. Other members of the subcommittee were John Foster Dulles (chairman), Hamilton Fish Armstrong, Philip C. Jessup, and Walter Lippmann. The book bears, however, the unmistakable stamp of the rapporteur.

[34] Carr's *Twenty Years' Crisis* (London, 1939) and Dunn's *Peaceful Change* differed in essential respects. Carr's book was published after the Munich settlement and could be interpreted as a defense of the appeasement policies of the Chamberlain government. Dunn's book had by no means the same prescriptive implications.

[35] *A Working Peace System* (London, 1944).

[36] *Peaceful Change*, 51.

[37] *Ibid.*, 127-28.

for change through the available procedures of diplomacy, arbitrations, conferences, international legislation, and the League of Nations. About these procedures, he concluded: "The notable thing about them is that they are voluntary procedures. The things to be changed, on the other hand, are for the most part things which are highly valued and not willingly given up by existing holders. This fact cannot be disguised by any multiplication of specific institutions and techniques for dealing with demands for change. The widespread notion that by the mere calling of conferences, the establishment of international commissions of inquiry or the devising of new techniques of negotation it will be possible to find acceptable solutions for all demands for change is largely the product of wishful thinking. It is useless to pile up additional institutions unless they take full account of existing values and attitudes which determine national policies." [38]

In 1940 Frederick S. Dunn succeeded Spykman as director of the Yale Institute. For the rest of his life, he subordinated his own research and writing interests to those of Yale Institute (and later Princeton Center of International Studies) colleagues.

He continued to believe in and encourage policy-oriented research, and as problems of national security became central with the onset of the Second World War, Institute studies were more and more focused on the making and improvement of national security policy. Dunn did not believe, however, that the denizens of the ivory tower ought to try to do the diplomatist's job. Public officials would always have superior access to current information and had the responsibility of making decisions. Private scholars, on the other hand, could examine problems and procedures on a longer time-scale or in a broader framework, and had the opportunity and the responsibility of completing their research before they reported on its results.

Institute studies were "primarily devoted to clarifying problems in the foreign policy of the United States." [39] They were, one should note, designed to clarify, not to settle, problems. He was still trying to improve national policy-making rather than to make policy from offstage; but as Director of the Yale Institute he was stalking bigger game than the legal officer in a twentieth-cenury Foreign Office.

---

[38] *Ibid.,* 125.

[39] Each volume in the series contained this phrase in its frontmatter, as did volumes in the later series of the Princeton Center of International Studies.

Dunn was insistent that Institute studies be "policy-oriented" in the sense that they ask questions the answers to which make a difference. He wanted improved decisions in foreign affairs, and this meant providing the decision-maker and the scholar with deeper understanding and better analytical tools.

The Institute was not hierarchically organized. Directives as to research tasks did not simply flow down from the top. The Yale Institute was organized more as "a band of brothers"; indeed, in the general description of the Institute's publications which appeared in each of the monographs after 1944 there was the statement: "The members of the Institute work at all times in close association, but each member is free to formulate his research projects in his own way and each published study represents an individual analysis of a problem." [40]

Institute members, who occupied adjacent offices, had easy access to each other. They met together one afternoon a week for informal but focused discussion. They frequently lunched together. They read each other's draft manuscripts. This was the antithesis of programmed research. Yet the leadership of the Director was not questioned. His evaluation of research priorities provided the basis for foundation support. His decisions in recruiting research personnel influenced the direction and quality of the research. It was his probing questions and marginal comments on draft manuscripts that largely held the Institute members to the central task of advancing knowledge relative to the control and improvement of policy-making in foreign affairs.

What did he see as significant questions worthy of being answered by Institute research? In general, there were two kinds of questions—those relating to major changes in the world political environment and those relating to the foreign policy process. Studies of geopolitical relations between the New World and the Old, of Soviet-Western relations, of the prospect for the development of China as a first-ranking power, of the demands of colonial peoples in the postwar world, of Britain's role as a junior partner in the Atlantic system, of the Soviet view of the United States, and of the impact of atomic power upon world politics fall into the first cate-

---

[40] See, for example, p. ii of Percy E. Corbett, *Law and Society in the Relations of States* (New York, 1951). This volume, the last published under Institute auspices, before the Institute was disbanded in 1951, has a complete list of Institute monographs on the same page.

gory.[41] Studies of the role of law in international relations, of the role of Congress in foreign policy, and of public opinion and foreign policy fall into the second.[42]

"Facts" by themselves had little interest for Dunn. He wanted lean, well-written books which an intelligent but very busy practitioner in the field of foreign affairs would still find time to read. He preferred short books and set an example for his colleagues in this respect. He wished to see published only the data necessary to support the conclusions and only the conclusions relevant to improved policy. As Institute director, Dunn took his editorial responsibilities very seriously. He believed that clear writing reflected lucid thinking.

He also believed in removing other possible obstacles to communicating with his target audience, what today might be called "the foreign affairs community." It included the decision-makers themselves as well as international relations scholars and elements of the attentive public. One way to reach this community was through the Yale Institute memorandum series. The memoranda were mimeographed and usually longer than journal articles but too short to stand alone as books. They were sent to persons in and out of government who had prior knowledge of and had expressed interest in the work of the Yale Institute or in its memorandum series. They were distributed partly to elicit helpful reactions to interim reports on research, but perhaps even more to get into the hands of the Institute's target audience timely and compact studies.

A second way to improve communications within the foreign affairs community was via *World Politics,* begun as a quarterly journal at Yale in 1948. It was intended to be an academic journal which would avoid reliance either on "big names" or excessive topicality to win readers. Professor Dunn wanted it to be attractive both as to content and format to practitioners and scholars alike. On the more important question of content, he sought to develop and apply criteria of inclusion and exclusion which would give

---

[41] By Nicholas J. Spykman, William T. R. Fox, David N. Rowe, Annette B. Fox, Percy E. Corbett, Frederick C. Barghoorn, and Bernard Brodie, respectively.

[42] By Percy E. Corbett, Robert A. Dahl, and Gabriel A. Almond, respectively.

shape to the emerging study of international relations. His focus was on the political process in the absence of central authority.[43]

It was a deliberate choice that the new journal should be named *World Politics,* to emphasize that it was not just the relations of hypostatized states but a world political process acting primarily through governments which was being studied. It followed that Professor Dunn persisted in his interest in those studies of the process which clarified the choices of men in government. It also followed that the test of relevance was the question being asked rather than the source of the data being analyzed or the technique of analysis being used.

His own writing in the first years after World War II demonstrated his continuing attention to the conditions favoring harmonization of apparently conflicting national interests. In *The Absolute Weapon,* for example, his essay on "The Common Problem" is a sensitive examination of the circumstances which would permit a treaty for the international control of atomic energy to bear the load put upon it by any temptations to violate it.[44] In *War and the Minds of Men*[45] he saw a new international arena in the struggle for the hearts and minds of men on a "middle ground between the bargaining of diplomats and total war." The book reflected both the keenness of his interest in discovering alternatives to two-way atomic war and his receptivity to the findings of all the social sciences, especially including social psychology, that would point toward better ways of attaining broad policy objectives.[46]

Dunn never confused being receptive to the findings of sociology and psychology with uncritical acceptance of the policy prescrip-

---

[43] "International relations," Dunn wrote, "is concerned with the questions that arise in the relations between autonomous political groups in a world system in which power is not centered at one point."—"The Scope of International Relations," *World Politics,* I (October 1943), 144.

[44] Bernard Brodie, ed., *The Absolute Weapon* (New York, 1946), 3-17. In this essay Mr. Dunn was exemplifying in a special case a point of view he had long held about international law in general. "International law," he had earlier written, "is in the last analysis nothing more than a sociological mechanism for making smooth the path of intercourse between nations and providing a solvent for their conflicting interests. This being the case, the proper approach to a study of it would seem to be according to the nature and subject matter of the relationships it is intended to regulate. These relationships are more or less clearly defined social phenomena, and are not derived from the fundamental rights of nations around which the present system of classification seeks to group them."—Review of Charles G. Fenwick, *International Law* (New York, 1924), in *Columbia Law Review,* XXV (November, 1925), 983.

[45] New York, 1950.

[46] See especially *ibid.,* Chapters 3-5.

tions of those who believed that "tensions are a kind of malignant growth in the minds of people which can be cut out by some form of mental surgery." He saw them rather as "symptoms of deeper conditions, which must be understood before they can be removed."[47] "It is not very useful," he wrote, "to talk about what might be done with men's minds if only some inconvenient features of present world politics could be ignored. Daydreaming about some other world than the one in which it is necessary to operate seldom opens any doors to successful action."[48] As an adviser to the American delegation at a series of UNESCO conferences, Professor Dunn gained a clear view of the choices which had to be made through that organization in a divided world so different from that foreseen by UNESCO's founders. His analysis was accordingly directed to the needs of men who had to decide how to work through UNESCO under the conditions of the cold war.

The reincarnation of the Yale Institute as the Princeton Center of International Studies in 1951 involved no sharp break in the patterns or directions of research. The country's dependence on preparedness rather than potential for security in the atomic age meant more emphasis than ever on politico-military studies and on studies of peacetime coalition arrangements such as NATO.[49] The new requirement for intelligent decisions about the Afro-Asian world and the developing areas generally was reflected in more research on comparative politics.[50]

On the other hand, men working at the Princeton Center have shown a concern for highly abstract problems in theory which was uncharacteristic of the Yale group. In part, this reflects the historical discontinuities of the thermonuclear era. Model-building and "hypothetical history" take the place of historical analogy. In part, it reflects the broad tolerance of Professor Dunn as Director. At Princeton as at Yale he was quite willing to see members of his research group formulate their own research program. In part, it reflected his recognition that, in spite of his own interest in the patient examination of case histories of officials in action, "the cure for the disease is quite often found far from the site of the epidemic."

---

[47] *Ibid.*, 110.
[48] *Ibid.*, 94.
[49] See, for example, the studies of Klaus Knorr and William W. Kaufmann.
[50] See, for example, the studies of Gabriel A. Almond, Lucian W. Pye, and Myron Weiner.

Frederick S. Dunn's own research at Princeton was along lines wholly consistent with his earlier inquiries. With a small group of colleagues he undertook to describe and evaluate the steps in the making of the Japanese peace settlement. In recognition of the increasing importance of democratic control of foreign affairs, one resulting volume concentrates on the domestic political process as it impinges on the decision-maker in foreign affairs.[51] Professor Dunn's own book, *Peace-making and the Settlement with Japan*, to be posthumously published in 1963, takes more specific account of the way in which responsible officials, and particularly John Foster Dulles, handled the stream of information flowing to them from the outside world. In this case, as in all the others on which he had worked, he was not interested in the case for its own sake but in asking, "What is this a case of?" and in discovering "what wisdom can be distilled out of it." [52]

How important Professor Dunn's work has been may be judged from his own writings and those of his Yale and Princeton colleagues. It remains only to notice two remarkable ways in which his scholarly leadership was publicly recognized. There is first the way in which his Yale Institute became a model for others to follow. It cannot be accidental that the present directors of four academic international relations research groups were all Yale colleagues of Frederick S. Dunn.[53] The second evidence is the recognition of his work by his alma mater, Princeton University, which gave him an honorary Doctor of Laws degree in 1949 and two years later, in an almost unprecedented act of confidence, invited him to return as Albert G. Milbank Professor of International Law and Practice and to bring with him no less than six of his Yale Colleagues.

Frederick Sherwood Dunn listed in a *World Politics* article as some "important emerging trends in research in international relations" the shifts from reformism to realism, from the study of formal structures to the study of informal process, from single-factor

---

[51] Bernard C. Cohen, *The Political Process and Foreign Policy* (Princeton, 1957).

[52] *Peace-making and the Settlement with Japan*, Introduction, xviii.

[53] Max Millikan, Director of the Center for International Studies at the Massachusetts Institute of Technology; Arnold Wolfers, Director of the Washington Center of Foreign Policy Research associated with Johns Hopkins University; Klaus Knorr, Director of the Center of International Studies at Princeton University; and William T. R. Fox, Director of the Institute of War and Peace Studies at Columbia University.

to multiple-factor explanations, from abstract speculation to systematic observations, from the study of inter-state relations to the study of world politics, and from implicitly assumed to explicitly analyzed goals.[54] He was writing in capsule form his own intellectual biography.

---

[54] "The Present Course of International Relations Research," *World Politics*, II (October, 1949), 81-95.

IV

THEORIES AS FORCES IN MODERN WORLD POLITICS

From *The Role of Theory in International Relations* (Van Nostrand, 1964)

I shall begin this discussion by making an arbitrary distinction between the body of disciplined writing by the serious disinterested professional student of international relations, which we call "international relations theory,"[1] and the much larger body of writing, much of it propagandistic, which demonstrates "theories of international relations" held by men whose attitudes may be significant for world politics. A comprehensive theory of international relations would take full account of the luxuriating proliferation of theories or perspectives which mold policy and govern action.

It is possible to construct a model of world politics in which only states appear as actors and in which state actions conform to criteria of rationality specified by the elaborator of the model. There would be no room in this model for the theories to operate except as a way of accounting for deviations from "rational" state behavior. Such a model has many virtues. Not the least is that it spares the observer of actual world politics the temptation, every time he comes upon some purely expediential state action taken in apparently rational pursuit of self-interest narrowly defined, to stop and denounce it. It has, however, some limitations. It often does not

[1] For example, 'The International System," *World Politics,* Vol. XIV, No. 1 (October, 1961).

serve to explain why a given state followed one particular selfish line of action rather than another when the two were apparently equally plausible in terms of the theory. Furthermore, it may not be very useful in explaining why apparently irrational actions or inexplicable miscalculations so often occur.

It is probably this kind of incompleteness which led Arnold Wolfers to assert the need for what he called a two-angled theory of international relations.[2] Thus he sees as a future task the construction of a super-theory in which so-called "minds of men" theories and decision-making theories of international relations are integrated with theories which focus exclusively on relations among states. In another of his writings, Professor Wolfers has advanced a hypothesis regarding the difference between Anglo-American and Continental European approaches toward foreign affairs.[3] He finds the contrast to be between what he calls a philosophy of choice and a philosophy of necessity. However much or little choice there may in fact have been, the vigor of the debate and the continuing tradition of dissent are evidence of belief in its existence and seem to have shaped both British and American foreign policy in ways which A. J. P. Taylor[4] has brilliantly documented so far as the British are concerned.

This Anglo-American philosophy of choice is one element of a syndrome of perspectives which I have elsewhere described as the "liberal-civilian mind" on civil-military relations and national security policy.[5] Men who shared this set of perspectives often thought of preparedness for war as resting upon a self-confirming hypothesis. They believed that he who prepared for war, because he expects war, helps thereby to bring on war. They tended to think of organized armed forces in peace, particularly standing armies, as providing more of an internal threat to the nation's liberties than they do an external protection for those liberties. Some of them, both on the Left and on the Right, brushed aside the European balance of power as an idea invented by people with a vested in-

[2] Arnold Wolfers, "The Actors in International Politics," *Theoretical Aspects of International Relations* (W. T. R. Fox, ed.) (Notre Dame, Ind.: University of Notre Dame Press, 1959), pp. 83-106.

[3] Arnold Wolfers and Laurence W. Martin (eds.), *The Anglo-American Tradition in Foreign Affairs* (New Haven, Conn.: Yale University Press, 1956).

[4] *The Troublemakers* (London: H. Hamilton, 1957).

[5] William T. R. Fox, "Diplomatists and Military People," *Diplomacy in a Changing World* (S. D. Kertesz and M. A. Fitzsimons, eds.) (Notre Dame, Ind.: University of Notre Dame Press, 1959), pp. 35-54; and "Representativeness and Efficiency: Dual Problem of Civil-Military Relations," *Political Science Quarterly*, LXXVI, No. 3 (September, 1961), 354-366.

terest in arms races or in foreign meddling. Others did not think of the military at all most of the time and would have achieved a kind of invincible civilian supremacy by remaining so ignorant of military requirements that there would rarely be a temptation to vote the armed services enough funds so they could be strong enough to threaten either the internal order or the external foe. This combination of beliefs was in the nineteenth century by no means as foolish as it sounds in the context of today's world politics; for in Britain to some extent, and in the United States to a very great extent, during most of the nineteenth century national security was a premise of public policy and not a goal. The English Channel and the Atlantic Ocean made Britain and America respectively "islands" in relation to the strife of Europe. Secure from the possibility of quick defeat by invasion in a short war, there was little need for much peacetime military policy. As the facts of world politics changed in the twentieth century, however, the liberal-civilian mind found itself ill-equipped to meet the urgent threats to American liberties which came from foreign governments whose appetite for dominance over ever-widening areas was seemingly insatiable.

Systematic studies of perspectives which mold policy affecting foreign relations have been quite numerous in the past decade. Nathan Leites has attempted to codify the behavior patterns of the Politburo.[6] Pamela Wrinch has endeavored to show that there are certain consistencies of objectives, of attitude, of method of calculating the correct course of action which are to be found throughout the whole sixty-year span of Winston Churchill's public life.[7] Warner Schilling has studied the images of world politics held by American admirals in World War I and those of American scientists since World War II.[8] Parenthetically, I may note that the admirals had a view of world politics which resembled that of Charles Beard more than it did that of the so-called power school of international relations. Beard and the admirals both believed

---

[6] Nathan Leites, *A Study of Bolshevism* (Glencoe, Ill.: The Free Press, 1953).

[7] Pamela Wrinch, "The Military Strategy of Winston Churchill," Studies in Political Science Series, Boston University, 1961, No. 5; and "Sir Winston Churchill on the Military Requirements of Great Britain," *Public Policy: The Yearbook of the Graduate School of Public Administration* (Cambridge, Mass.: Harvard University Press, 1958), pp. 151-169.

[8] Warner R. Schilling, "Civil-Naval Politics in World War I," *World Politics*, VII, No. 4 (July, 1955), 572-591; and "Scientists, Foreign Policy and Politics," *The American Political Science Review*, LVI, No. 2 (June, 1962), pp. 287-300 (also printed in Robert Gilpin and Christopher Wright, eds., *Scientists and National Policy Making*, New York, Columbia University Press, 1964). The World War I study is being expanded into a full-length monograph.

that conflicts over trade routes bring naval powers into conflict. Beard drew the conclusion that the game was not worth the candle, that navies cost more than the prospective profits from the trade which they were supposed to be protecting.[9] The admirals, however, accepted the desirability of foreign trade as given and do not ever seem to have set the cost of protecting that trade against the gain from having it. Today, advancing science and technology are great semi-independent variables in the equations of world politics; scientists, perhaps even more than admirals of another era, are in positions close to the center of decision-making in our national government. There is a new interest in understanding the attitudes of these scientists, who find themselves called upon to give technical advice and do so in a way that has inevitable political overtones.[10]

A. J. P. Taylor's *The Troublemakers* serves to remind us that the student of theories of international relations must keep himself aware of the attitudes of men who may form alternative governments, and even of the smaller group who are dissenters in the opposition party. Yesterday's Dissent may be tomorrow's Orthodoxy. Bertrand Russell's recent slogan, "Better Red than dead," suggests how much difference it would make if that attitude were even more widespread in England than it already is. Henri Spaak is pressing hard for European integration on terms which would provide adequate protection for his native Belgium; it is, though, Europe the bloc actor and not just Belgium the national actor whose actions must be illuminated by a comprehensive body of international relations theory.

I have said that the truth or falsity of a given perspective on world politics is not directly correlated with the strength of a given theory as a force. The Protocol of the Elders of Zion, for example, was important though it was the most obvious nonsense. This Protocol is not, of course, by itself a theory, but its asserted existence lent plausibility to the belief that the wire-pullers in this world are a Jewish conspiracy. The truth or falsity of particular theories may, however, have a great deal to do with what consequences flow from action in accordance with the theory. False theories may well drive a state to disaster.

---

[9] Cf. Charles A. Beard, *The Idea of National Interest* (New York: Macmillan, 1934) and *Open Door at Home* (New York: Macmillan, 1935).

[10] Robert G. Gilpin, Jr., *American Scientists and Nuclear Weapons: The Intra-Scientific Conflict Over Nuclear Weapons Policy* (Princeton, N. J.: Princeton University Press, 1962).

Excessively obsolete theories may fail to take account of major transformations in world politics, such as have been occurring with bewildering variety in this century—for example, the new role of the Afro-Asian nations in a state system which has expanded from being European to being a world system and in which the forces of nationalism are multiplying sovereignties in the non-European world; the new role of public opinion in the conduct of foreign relations in the Europeanized world at a time when the sphere of state action is so broad as to have strained the capacity of the old foreign policy elites; the emergence of bloc actors in a world of bipolar competition and intercontinental strategic air and missile power; and the breakdown of a sharp distinction between peace and every form of war but two-way thermonuclear exchange. Thus, old-style theorists of collective security assumed that irretrievably decisive events would not take place before the economic and military pressures of the international community could be mobilized and applied.[11] To take a quite different example of obsolete perspectives, President de Gaulle still writes as if France were a first-ranking power in a Europe-centered world of nation-state actors.[12]

Excessively simple or deterministic theories may artifically constrict the range of choice of the policy maker. The theorists who assume that there are really only two powers in the world today, that only nuclear weapons count, that retaliatory capabilities are unlikely to deter, and that conflict is unbridgeable leave open only two bleak alternatives—the catastrophe of thermonuclear war and the humiliation of Western surrender.[13]

[11] There are technological as well as political reasons why Articles 43 and 48 of the United Nations Charter remain a dead letter, for only military planning against an identified possible aggressor seems to make sense in the era in which the greatest war may be a very short war.

[12] See, for example, his call for the organization of Western defense on a basis of national forces rather than of integrated forces and his statement that sovereign states are "the only entities that have the right to obey and to be obeyed" which was made at a news conference at the Elyseé Palace (*New York Times*, September 6, 1960).

[13] A decade ago, Harold D. Lasswell could properly assume that it was primarily the Soviet policy maker whose expectations of "inevitable" war so constricted his view of the range of choice that this expectation was a self-confirming hypothesis (" 'Inevitable' War: A Problem in the Control of Long-Range Expectations," *World Politics*, Vol. II, No. 1 [October, 1949], 1-39). In the 1960's, the Soviet call for "peaceful coexistence" may not be sounding a retreat in ultimate Soviet objectives, but it is a step in transforming the expectation of inevitable short-run victory in war into an undated expectation of final triumph in a millenial future. Meanwhile, there are some Americans who continue to attribute to the Soviet government a combination of intentions and capabilities that cuts away any middle ground between total victory and total surrender.

Excessively voluntaristic theories may, when the inevitable disappointment occurs, trigger a reaction of ignorant cynicism. Those, for example, who had seen the United Nations as offering an avenue of escape from something called power politics, may be too easily disenchanted with the reality, in which the United Nations is an arena for intergreat-power rivalry and an instrument for registering the new importance of the new Afro-Asian nations.

One particular form of excessive voluntarism is excessive group privatization, characterized by extreme isolationism and rationalized by a belief that what goes on in the rest of the world can have no harmful effect on the "private" affairs of the self-isolating nation.[14] It is doubtful whether many of the privatized groups have any articulated theory regarding foreign affairs at all. A set of perspectives, however, which excludes from conscious consideration any reference to the world beyond the limits of the national homeland had within it an implicit theory, namely, that such harm as may come from outside is sufficiently slight so that the nation can choose to ignore it.[15]

Let us return now to the question of the relation between a theory of international relations and the various perspectives or theories which I have just characterized as privatized, partial, obsolete, simplistic, too voluntaristic, too involuntaristic, and so on. The most primitive and inchoate of these perspectives are in fact little more than moods. Mass moods may not be directly relevant to understanding the foreign policies of many countries; however, in Western constitutional democracies generally and in the United States in particular, where democratic institutions and practices antedate any fixed traditions of foreign policy, the moods of large sections of the public may effectively restrict the range of choice open to those formally charged with responsibility for foreign policy. Gabriel Almond has described these moods and contrasted them with the more highly articulated perspectives of opinion elites in and out of government.[16]

My concern, however, is not so much with those who are governed by moods alone as it is with those who advance theories re-

[14] "Group privatization" is a phrase which I owe to Nathan Leites, "Trends in Moral Temper." *The American Imago*, 5 (1948), 3-37.

[15] This is occasionally made explicit. Robert Welch, the founder of the John Birch society, shares with most other right-wing extremists a belief that domestic communism is more of a threat than Soviet military power and has even referred to the American military effort in the 1960's as "wasteful . . . a phony defense against an external enemy" (*Newsweek*, December 4, 1961, p. 4).

[16] *The American People and Foreign Policy* (New York: Harcourt, 1950).

garding politics, including world politics, which are explicitly meant to be relevant to policy choices and with those who consciously accept such theories. When the Aldermaston marchers march or the venerable Lord Russell sits down in Trafalgar Square to win support for a "sane" nuclear weapons policy, they are reflecting more than a mood. They reflect a thought-through view of world politics, even though it be a view which rests on premises that most students of world politics would not regard as tenable and some would regard as absurd.

The Aldermaston marchers and British pacifists generally, the Marxists who believe that foreign policy serves the interests of the ruling classes far more effectively than it does the exploited masses, those who accept the somewhat passé and historically inaccurate analyses of imperialism first expounded by Hobson and later by Lenin have one common characteristic, however they may otherwise differ: they operate on the basis of simplified and largely deterministic views of the world political process. These are not the only simplifiers. I have already referred to those who accept the authenticity of the Protocol of the Elders of Zion and to those who believe that "this is the Age of the Big Two, and two cannot stay in balance." The simplest of all are the "single-shot, grand design" utopians who say, "Take my prescription and the world is saved. Otherwise all is lost." Those who believe that Utopia can be achieved only on a piecemeal basis, but believe nevertheless that progress is inevitable, are also simplifiers; and so are those with an irrational faith in the powers of rationality. For the moment, I am not concerned with the question of the extent to which some of the oversimplified prescriptions which are advanced as total prescriptions may not in fact have a certain relevance if more modestly put forward as partial prescriptions. My concern is with the effect on state behavior of belief in one or another unrealistically simplified explanation of world politics.

It is no doubt true that men who shared Woodrow Wilson's perspectives on world politics saw in far too simple terms the problem of establishing such a world order as would bring a millennium of peace to mankind. It is possible, however, that those who attribute the coming of World War II primarily to the failure of the League of Nations and therefore to the naïve perspectives of the Wilsonian peacemakers of 1919 also have far too simple a view of world politics. It was not just the League of Nations which failed. There was a failure of alliance policy, too. France and her East European allies became separated. Britain and France were unable to develop coordinated policies.[17] The Soviet Union and the Western powers each tried to turn Hitler's war back toward the other and accepted alliance with each other only when Hitler chose to make war in the East and in the West at the same time. The narrowly national security policies were as ill-conceived and ill-executed as the alliance policies and the collective security policies. Faith in France in the Maginot Line was as ill-justified as faith in Britain was in the strangling efficacy of economic warfare. Salvation was not in that period to be found *simply* by de-emphasizing "idealistic" international organization and re-emphasizing "realistic" military policies and alliance policies.

It is no criticism of E. H. Carr, the theorist, whose *Twenty Years' Crisis* is a landmark in modern international relations theory, to point out that E. H. Carr the publicist appears to have seen the episode of appeasement at Munich in 1938 as a triumph of British statesmanship and of the forces of prudence and moderation.[18] If, however, one refrains from attributing Mr. Carr's misreading of the meaning of Munich to some shortcoming in his theory of international relations, one ought to exercise a similar restraint with respect to the men Mr. Carr called utopians.

Neither the realists nor the utopians seem to have come off very well whenever they assumed that over-all foreign policy could be read directly from their particular over-all international relations theory. For example, in the interwar period both groups expected too much from the prescriptions based on their respective theories. The Wilsonians expected too much of the League, and some of their critics expected too much of appeasement. The one seemed to say, "We can create a world order in which the powerful, however wicked they may be, can be rendered harmless." The other seemed

[17] See Arnold Wolfers, *Britain and France Between Two Wars* (New York: Harcourt, 1940).

[18] It is a tribute to the enduring value of E. H. Carr's theoretical work that his *Twenty Years' Crisis* (New York: Macmillan, 1939) could appear as relevant in the postwar world as it had at the beginning of the war. Apart from the deletion of obsolete references to the events of Munich (pp. 278 and 282), the revised edition of 1946 required almost no change. The following is one deletion (p. 278) which is of particular significance for the purpose of the present analysis: "If the power relations of Europe in 1938 made it inevitable that Czecho-Slovakia should lose part of her territory, and eventually her independence, it was preferable (quite apart from any question of justice or injustice) that this should come about as the result of discussions round a table in Munich rather than as the result either of a war between the Great Powers or of a local war between Germany and Czecho-Slovakia." Query: Was it really "inevitable"? If not, were "discussions round a table" really preferable?

to say, "Hitler's Germany is powerful and becoming more powerful. It's too bad, but there's not much we can do about it."

It is not fair, and what is more important, it is not intellectually rewarding, to use the advent of World War II as a stick with which to beat either Woodrow Wilson or E. H. Carr. This does not mean, however, that prevailing climate of ideas has no relation to the "weather" of world politics. The avowed propagandist or revolutionary may be important in shaping the mass moods which set broad limits on the policy maker's effective range of choice. Their perspectives on world politics whether implicit or explicit need to be catalogued and analyzed. The impact of the dispassionate scholar may, on the other hand, be very great on that part of the attentive public most influential in making foreign policy choices and on the decision makers themselves, for it is their perspectives on world politics (or "theories" of international relations) which can be selectively modified in the direction of greater rationality. The remainder of this essay is accordingly devoted to examining the function of theory and the international relations theorists in refining the theories of policy-making elites and in improving the policy output.

An interwar generation of writing in which the tone was definitely optimistic, in which the possibility of the development of supranational institutions as a result of voluntary choice was portrayed as great, has been succeeded by a postwar generation in which the difficulties of creating world political institutions have been stressed and the tone of the writing is generally pessimistic. Between the Scylla of the excessive voluntarism of the first group and Charybdis of excessive involuntarism of the second, it is difficult to steer a prudent course. Hardly any of us believe that the future is wholly predetermined. Hardly any of us believe that we can make of the future anything we choose. If the attitudes of each of us were arranged along a continuum which stretches from a wholly predetermined future at one end of the continuum to absolute free will at the other, we would all be found rather far removed from either extreme.

The speculative writings of such men as Reinhold Niebuhr, E. H. Carr, Nicholas J. Spykman and Hans J. Morgenthau have done a great deal to make untenable a position at one of these extremes.[19]

[19] See Niebuhr, *Moral Man and Immoral Society* (New York: Scribner, 1932) and *Christianity and Power Politics* (New York: Scribner, 1940); Carr, *op cit.*, Spykman, *America's Strategy in World Politics* (New York: Harcourt, 1942);

It is certainly not accidental that a theologian with a concern for social ethics, a Russian historian, a student of the sociology of conflict and of geopolitics, and a scholar with an earlier interest in international jurisprudence have demonstrated in their writings a convergence of intellectual interests and of moral concerns. How these interests and concerns have converged is carefully set forth in the recent book by Kenneth Thompson.[20] What kind of impact has this realist writing had on world politics and what kind can it have?

From the Thompson analysis, one can see more clearly than before what are the essential and discriminating elements in the body of writing which it is conventional today to call "realist." There are apparently two criteria by which one can distinguish this special kind of realism: an understanding that in world politics, as in domestic politics, human aspirations cannot be completely satisfied and that therefore politics must go on; and an understanding that other groups than one's own have interests and aspirations which must to some extent be satisfied if the intensity of the political competition is in any significant degree to be moderated. If these criteria are the litmus test of realist writing, terrible simplifiers like Marx and Haushofer have to be stricken from the list of realists; those who advocate as feasible the total victory of one side over the other fail to qualify. On the other hand, some scholars whom I have described elsewhere as "conscientious objectors in the Great Debate" may by this test turn out to be realists.[21] If the international relations theorist is to develop his subject so that it is most useful in the realm of public policy, distinctions and differences have to be thrashed out between men all of whom would be called realist by this system of classification. None of them has a view of the future which puts him at either extreme of the realist-utopian continuum.

Two world wars and a generation of realist writing have together deflated earlier hopes and expectations of world peace based on world government, or at least on a world organization enjoying the support of world opinion. Reference here is to the unwarranted ex-

---

and Morgenthau, *Scientific Man versus Power Politics* (Chicago: University of Chicago Press, 1946), in which the realist views on world politics of each of the four first attracted wide public attention.

[20] *Political Realism and the Crisis of World Politics* (Princeton, N. J.: Princeton University Press, 1960).

[21] William T. R. Fox, review of Thompson's *Political Realism and the Crisis of World Politics,* in *Union Seminary Quarterly Review,* Vol. XVI, No. 3 (March, 1961), 345-348.

pectations of those members of the lay public who have a naïve faith in simplistic prescriptions for an end to war, for a creation of supranational institutions, and for a beginning of universal and perpetual harmony. They almost certainly constitute a smaller proportion of the attentive public concerned with foreign affairs than they did a generation ago.

Scholars writing for a lay audience in the second half of the twentieth century will almost all agree that politics is a struggle for scarce values, that unlimited satisfaction is beyond everyone's reach, and that all-round moderation in trying to implement the policy objectives of one's own country makes for peace. Apart from these relatively undebatable propositions, what more has the international relations theorist to say to his fellow theorists and to the policy-making elites in need of benchmarks to guide them in their day-to-day activities?

Some of us may still have what others of us believe to be an unreasonable faith in our own powers of reason, but of course, nobody believes that anybody ought to have an unreasonable amount of faith in reason or anything else. The hard question turns out to be "Just how much faith in reason is reasonable?" Mos of us are realists in the sense that we have gained the maturity to know that progress is not inevitable and that man is not completely perfectible. But short of perfection, there are all kinds of degrees of optimism and pessimism regarding the direction and extent to which man can improve his present lot. Belief in how much progress, how rapidly, and in what direction constitutes evidence of immaturity.

Herbert Butterfield has stressed the requirement that the international relations scholar and the statesman, too, have a sense of history, that, in his words, they understand the necessity of co-operating with the historical process.[22] But does co-operation with the historical process mean total surrender, which is the way some people have interpreted E. H. Carr's *Twenty Years' Crisis* in the light of the coincidental advocacy of appeasement at Munich by the London *Times,* for which Mr. Carr was then writing? Kenneth Thompson has written that he agrees "with some of Carr's critics that he is sometimes blind to the . . . truth that there are occasions where reality must be brought into line with purpose." [23] If I understand his position, it is that man can and moral men should in

[22] Herbert Butterfield, *International Conflict in the Twentieth Century* (New York: Harper, 1960).
[23] Thompson, *op. cit.,* p. 28.

some measure be a master of his own destiny. I think our collective task is to identify much more precisely exactly what the occasions are which afford us the opportunity for mastering our destiny. Even though perfect rationality in our analyses may be beyond reach, and total satisfaction of our nation's foreign policy objectives as defined in the light of our private value preferences may also be far beyond reach, let us not confuse the demonstrable impossibility of being perfectly rational with the obvious possibility of being somewhat more rational than we have been. To return to my earlier metaphor, our task, after we have steered clear of the Scylla of excessive voluntarism, is as moral men to avoid being shipwrecked on the Charybdis of excessive involuntarism.

Because there is still a good deal of avoidable irrationality in the choices of policy makers and in the attitudes of the attentive public on foreign affairs, the social function of the international relations scholars, theorists included, is to induce greater rationality into the perspectives on world politics of those whose views shape public policy. Theory ought, therefore, to clarify choice within the range of genuine choice. It is irrational to sacrifice for a demonstrably unattainable goal, and it is sterile to argue over the desirability of non-existent choices. If this quest for greater rationality is carried on by men who have what Mr. Thompson has called "the saving grace of reciprocity," by men who understand that other nations and other men have interests and have a legitimate right to have interests, then theoretical activity ought to make for peace, too.

There has been very little attention paid in this essay to normative theories of international relations or to the normative aspects of mixed normative and empirical theories. Whatever may be the value preferences of elites and decision makers, the theory which the dispassionate, disinterested student of international relations is developing can have as its particular impact on modern world politics an increase in the rationality of the actions of the decision makers and in the attitudes of the public attentive to foreign affairs. Greater rationality in analysis and choice is likely to lead to a clarification of norms, and the clarification may in its turn cause some modifications in actual goals and preferences.

If the quest for greater rationality is undertaken by men whose "saving grace of reciprocity" permits them to tolerate as legitimate the interests of other groups and other nations who come to accept patterns of shared power as a basis for greater all-round security, then it is probable that the quest for rationality and the quest for peace will go hand in hand. But how, one may ask, can theoretical activity heighten rationality? In particular, how can the theoretical activity of the scholar heighten the rationality of men of influence in public policy? A short answer is that with the aid of theory facts can be better organized to portray the world in which political choices have to be made more accurately, to point to incompatibilities in policy goals and objectives which are being simultaneously pursued and thus point the way toward a reformulation which eliminates these incompatibilities, and to reveal more economical means for achieving stated ends. Theory can do this by developing the ordering concepts and the analytical models. Armed with this theory, the intellectual can transcend the limits of his own class, culture, and nation, or at any rate be more successful in doing this than without the theory.

Just as theory leads to the selection and ordering of the facts, so also facts can lead to elaboration of theory. Perspectives on world politics and particularly on the relation between the advanced countries of Europe and the Europeanized world and the colonial or underdeveloped areas could be put in a new theoretical framework once the anthropologist and sociologist had shattered the alleged factual basis for racist doctrines. Careful investigation of the influences which destroyed the so-called insularity of Britain and America from the politics of Continental Europe makes it easier to elaborate a theory of the relation between technological change and necessities for peacetime preparedness. Such analyses help to make it clear that under changed conditions, long-cherished policy objectives have to be supported by drastically changed military and diplomatic means.

Parenthetically, I should note that the same set of developments which undermined the basis of insularity in British and American policy also destroyed the basis for one of Joseph Stalin's most cherished doctrines, the doctrine of permanently operating factors. Carried to its logical extreme, this doctrine would have meant that the outcome of wars is not determined by the accident of the level of military preparedness at the moment the war begins or the particular pattern of development of forces that happens to exist at that time, but rather by such permanently operating factors as a superior social system. But the Soviet Union cannot persist in doctrines of insularity, either. The expectation that a big war would be a protracted war, leaving plenty of time for superior social systems and superior human and material resources to be mobilized and thrown into the struggle, has been destroyed for the Soviet side, too.

There may be some purely "art for art's sake" students of international relations, though I cannot name any. There are many who would describe a good deal of their own scholarly output as not being directly policy relevant, and in the short run not policy relevant at all. Richard Snyder and Morton Kaplan would be examples.[24] Many others have disciplined themselves to work on their chosen problems objectively and are prepared to accept as facts things which, as moral men, they would have preferred to have found to be otherwise. But there is a strong voluntaristic tradition in American scholarship in the social sciences generally, and in international relations particularly.[25] Compared to other countries, Americans who are teaching and researching and speculating in the field of international relations are many; they are industrious and they are well-supported. They work hard, and they are well-supported because both the scholar who is working in the field of international relations and the society which indulges him in his activity share a belief that the future is not wholly predetermined. Both believe that there are better and worse ways of coping with that future. Both believe that dispassionate investigation and teaching can be at least marginally significant in indicating the actual range of choice open to those who make policy and the differential consequences which flow from choosing one rather than another of the alternative courses of action.

The range of choice which is seen as open varies, both in degree and direction, with the school of thought. Thus a theoretical framework for the study of world politics in which great emphasis is put on the foundations of national power,[26] in which stress is laid on the distinctive intentions as well as the distinctive capabilities of each of the major actors or classes of actors in world politics, and in which stress is placed above all on the elements of strength and weakness in the power positions of various states—this theoretical framework is one in which the most significant choices appear to be those affecting the level and direction of a nation's military mobili-

---

[24] See Richard C. Snyder, H. W. Bruck, and Burton M. Sapin, *Decision Making as an Approach to the Study of International Relations* (Princeton, N. J.: Princeton University Press, 1954); and Morton A. Kaplan, *System and Process in International Politics* (New York: Wiley, 1957).

[25] See "The Teaching of International Relations in the United States" (with Annette Baker Fox), *supra*, pp. 14-35.

[26] See Harold Sprout and Margaret Sprout, *Foundations of National Power*, 2nd ed. (Princeton, N. J.: Van Nostrand, 1951).

zation and peacetime preparedness. On the other hand, a theoretical analysis in which the effort is concentrated on the discovery of uniformities in state behavior make it more likely that the truly critical areas of policy choice would be seen as lying outside the sector of defense policy, narrowly defined. Thus a theory which ascribes to each of the actors in the system a national interest and implicitly at least recognizes the legitimacy of each of these members of the state system in having interests provides the theoretical basis for examining opportunities for diplomacy, for negotiation, for compromise. Similarly, a legal analysis which focuses on problems of defining and protecting the rights of states, and of the interests which states are supposed to promote and maintain on behalf of the individuals who compose the state, is likely to illuminate areas of choice in international law and organization. Thus the contrast seems sharp between the theories of those who search for the distinctive attributes of each of the main actors in our state system and the theories of those who search for attributes generally shared by the actors in the system. It is less sharp between the theories of those who from a global point of view focus their speculation on the role of diplomacy in promoting national interests and the theories of those others who also from a global point of view seek to elaborate legal norms and organizational goals.

There is a need, if the international relations theorist is to play fully the role I have assigned to him of being a force for greater rationality in foreign policy-making, for correctives against excesses of involuntarism as well as against excesses of voluntarism. The problem is perhaps less acute with respect to long-run changes in world politics. It is hard to believe that the United States would not by the second half of the twentieth century have become one of the first-ranking powers of the world, whatever the powers of Europe might have done in the generation after the War Between the States. Britain and America alike, and perhaps Canada more than either, have reason to be thankful that the drastically changed Anglo-American relationship, which has resulted from the emergence of the United States as a world power, did not have to be established by an Anglo-American war.[27] The great transformations in world politics which are now under way, whether that caused by nuclear inventions or that by which the recently colonial areas

[27] Lionel Gelber has described in detail the critical decade in Anglo-American relations in his *Rise of Anglo-American Friendship* (London: Oxford University Press, 1938). In his subsequent writings, he has traced the expanding role of the United States in the Western alliance.

of the world have been making good their demands for independence, have to be accepted as facts. They cannot be reversed, and they cannot be wished away. The areas of critical choice may turn out to be those that concern not long-run change, but short-run change—and timing rather than the direction of action. Of course, it is possible for short-run consequences—for example, a failure to grasp an opportunity to reduce the chance of two-way thermonuclear war, or a failure to develop a national security policy which recognizes fully that irretrievably decisive events might come in the first hours of such a war if it did occur. With respect to short-run changes where the effort is to adapt to or to redirect but not to reverse the major transformations, theory ought to clarify questions of timeliness of action, of economy of means, of consistency of simultaneously pursued policies, of judgment in the light of imperfectly seen facts and incompletely understood objectives. Here is where the theorist can do perhaps more than he has so far done. By describing the long-run major transformations, he can set the frame within which the short-run choices are to be made. Divorced as he is from the superior sources of day-to-day information open to the decision makers charged with day-to-day decisions, he cannot always expect to write position papers as relevant as his colleague in government with more practical and immediate responsibilities and fuller information on the most recent events. However, he can establish guidelines.

He can, for example, increase the rationality of choice by indicating more economical ways of implementing objectives. Hot war is so much more costly in terms of the material and moral values of men than cold war that the highest priority should be given to the task of redefining apparently conflicting national interests so that these interests can so far as possible be harmonized. Whether by diplomacy or by some integration of interests in a larger transnational organization or expanded corpus of international law, the task is urgent.

International relations theory may have an impact upon those charged with responsibility for public policy different from that which it has on those who provide unofficial leadership for influential opinion groups. Both groups need the ordered understanding of modern world politics which comes from being able to distinguish what one observes from what one finds it convenient to observe, and from being able to select and arrange facts about world politics in a theoretical framework which facilitates dispassionate judgment. For the professional military man, the diplomatist, the scientist, the industrial mobilizer, the legislator, and top officials of the government—men with the sobering responsibility of actual choice—the role of theory is, however, not primarily to act as a corrective for a Marx or a Mackinder or a Machiavelli or the various contemporary simplifiers of the Right and the Left. It is to make it easier for the conscientious public servant in or out of uniform, elective or appointed, to act with a greater awareness of his particular role and that of others charged with somewhat different tasks.

In a period of long lead-times the soldier is apt to want to plan for a set future. He complains that the State Department cannot make up its mind. The diplomatist meanwhile is apt to want to keep the future open in order to try to maximize the chances of peace by working on the opponent's intentions as well as on improving his own nation's capabilities. The scientist, unlike the soldier, has not been schooled by long tradition to respect what the soldier calls civilian supremacy; it could be more appropriately called politician supremacy. "Politics" may in fact be a dirty word, an epithet used to characterize the behavior of those elected officials who do not accept proffered scientific advice. Not all influential scientists have yet learned to preface statements on public policy with the phrase, "Speaking from a purely scientific point of view," in the way that senior military men have long prefaced their statements with the phrase, "Speaking from a purely military point of view." So the scientist may not always have disciplined himself or been disciplined to keep clear the extent to which his policy advice is grounded exclusively in scientific considerations and the extent to which it is grounded in incompletely examined political premises. Like other experts called to advise the politicians who in our democratic system have the ultimate responsibility for policy, he too, can play a more effective part by being aware of the distinctive roles of those contributors to the making of foreign policy and national security policy whose contributions are based on an expertise quite different from his own. Some of these politicians have greater sophistication about the world political process than he, or at any rate a longer experience at attempting to be sophisticated.

It is only by gaining a whole view of policy that the participant with responsibility for one part or skill to analyze that part gains either self-awareness or a sympathetic awareness of the problems of those with other skills and responsibilities. Of course, it is even more important for those at the topmost political levels to have such a whole view, so as to be able to orchestrate the sometimes conflicting advices from their diverse technical experts.[28] But what kind of knowledge enables one to transcend the bias inherent in his own particular narrow skill and responsibility and in his natural preference to act on the basis of means with whose use he is best acquainted, or that inherent in his loyalty to the particular organization—whether military or civilian—of which he is a part and his natural preference to act through the familiar organization?

One way is to gain greater awareness of the attitudes distinctive to various participants in national security policy-making, so one can then decide how appropriate these attitudes are to the job in hand. Thus, the diplomatist who comes to understand why the soldier feels he needs to plan for a set future can deal more intelligently with Pentagon exhortations to "Make up your mind."

What are some of these differences of attitude? It depends somewhat on one's theory of international relations how one asks the questions, and somewhat on the answers how one reformulates the theory. State behavior can, at least in the short run, be explained in terms of the perspectives of a relatively small number of people.

Is it by building up strength or by demonstrating nonprovocative intentions that one expects to control the behavior of a prospective opponent? In building up strength, is the emphasis on deterring a war or winning it if it comes? What loss in deterrent capacity would one accept to preserve an advantage in actual war if one maintained the secrecy of one's secret weapon? How closely geared ought the pattern of peacetime preparedness be to foreign policy objectives specified by the Foreign Office? How much reliance may be placed on the armed strength of one's allies over what time period? What limitations on military means ought to be accepted to keep a local war local if these limitations seem to prevent quick or decisive victory? Is war when it comes seen as a crusade or as a continuation of policy? How much sacrifice of military efficiency is acceptable in order that sacrifice may be more equitably distributed and how much otherwise legitimate secrecy so that democracy may function?

When one has planned for the single worst contingency, World War III, what more is there to do? Does one tailor his military means to given foreign policy ends, or shape his foreign policy ends

[28] Schilling, *loc. cit.*

to available military means? How are calculations regarding the prospective opponent's intentions allowed to influence the estimate of military requirements? Is the future seen as set, with the main allies and the main opponents known? Is the goal of security seen as objectively definable and its attainment as a problem capable of solution with objective precision?

Is there a tendency to view delay and qualified actions as evidence of indecision and weakness or as evidence of willingness to let time work for one's own side? Are long-run considerations weighed heavily or lightly in short-run decisions? With what degree of candor and willingness are political considerations allowed to transform technical problem-solving into agonizing political choosing? At what point ought political debate to stop and experts begin to issue orders? How ought a political superior to deal with conflicting expert advice?

I am not suggesting that a theory of international relations can provide answers to all these questions, especially because so many of them have a normative component. But a theory has to take account of the range of answers that men in high places have by their words and by their action given to these, and to many other questions I might have raised which are less directly focused on problems of national security. With perspectives codified and recurrent behavior patterns noted, the implicit theories of some of the human actors in international relations can be made more explicit. The model of a world of state actors acting rationally to maximize values imputed to these abstract entities can be refined to account for what might otherwise be seen as idiosyncratic deviations. Meanwhile, making implicit theories explicit may turn some of them into self-disconfirming hypotheses and may thus promote a firmer and more rational consensus among those who must make the day-to-day-decisions on foreign policy.

Theory then is the tool by which we can identify and evaluate the perspectives on modern world politics which we have called "theories"—the perspectives both of policy makers within the government and the attentive public without. In so doing, we can improve the theory; by clarifying both ends and means, we can improve foreign policy, too.

V

THE USES OF INTERNATIONAL RELATIONS THEORY[1]

From *Theoretical Aspects of International Relations* [University of Notre Dame Press, 1959]

I

Why should anyone expect an international relations theorist to be useful? Isn't his function to be omniscient and disinterested? The answer to the second question provides the answer to the first. By not allowing his interests to cloud his vision, the student of international relations can make the observations of world politics which permit him to advance disinterested theories to account for and explain these observations. Thus, these disinterested conclusions help the policy-maker act with greater rationality to implement his values.

The scholar's interest ought not to influence his observations or his conclusions, but it certainly influences his selection of problems. Thus, the greater the value consensus between the theorist and the policy-maker, the greater the use of theory to policy. Given this value consensus, it is difficult for a social scientist to discover a

[1] This essay was first published in a symposium volume, *Theoretical Aspects of International Relations* (Notre Dame, Ind., University of Notre Dame Press, 1959), which I edited. It and the other essays in the volume were originally prepared for an inter-university seminar on international relations theories which met at Columbia University during 1956 and 1957 under the auspices of its Institute of War and Peace Studies. A grant from the Rockefeller Foundation made the seminar possible.—W. T. R. F.

problem worthy of his concentrated effort at solution which is not policy-relevant. Debate about the use of international relations studies often turns on whether or not research and theorizing ought to be "policy-oriented." This is largely a false issue.

Let us examine some speculative or theoretical analyses in order to demonstrate their actual or potential policy relevance. E. H. Carr's *The Twenty Years' Crisis,* first published in 1930, counsels against those who try hard to buck the tides of history. For Carr, policy is seen as skillful adjustment, with the fewest broken heads possible, to the basic changes that are going to take place in world politics anyway. It is good advice, and is thus broadly policy-relevant, for those with too much zeal and too little humility as to the possibility of man becoming master of his own destiny. No more than any other general analysis ought it to have been used as a device for reading over-all policy directly from one's general theory of world politics. When it was first published in the months after the Munich crisis, it was possible to read this pioneering analysis as a polemical document in the appeasement debate. This, however, is a misuse of international relations theory, for it would have taken extensive and detailed analysis of the European political scene at the time of the Munich crisis, and possibly even the advantage of hindsight, to show whether the policy of the Chamberlain government was skillful adjustment or surrender of the most fundamental national interest.

More specifically policy-oriented was Nicholas J. Spykman's *America's Strategy in World Politics.*[2] Professor Spykman was in fact shooting at a moving target. His manuscript took shape during a period in which the Nazi menace over Europe after June 1940 had shaken the confidence of even the staunchest isolationist in America's capacity to stand alone. The isolationist then often adopted one of two variants of his isolationist position, quarter-sphere defense or hemisphere defense. It was this particular midsummer madness to which Spykman addressed himself. He assumed the existence of a two-state world, the Old World and the New World, and then demonstrated to his own satisfaction that the Old could conquer the New. If, he concluded, you do not want that to happen, you must, to the extent necessary, intervene in the Old World to prevent its being dominated by some one power or combination of powers. By the time the book was published, the attack at Pearl Harbor had cut off public debate in the United

[2] New York, 1942.

States about the merits of intervention. The Spykman book was not, however, without effect. Not only did this and similar works help to define the meaning of the war effort into which the United States had with every show of reluctance been dragged, but they helped to deflate in advance some of the exaggerated expectations as to what victory would bring. Thus, the Spykman type of analysis, like that of Carr, helped to clarify choice by limiting it.

The result of social science theorizing is not always to constrict the range of choice which official and other influential elites see as open to them. In delimiting the possible for those who must select a course of action, the theorist may also shed light on recently proposed policy alternatives and sometimes even direct attention to courses of action previously unimagined or imagined to be impossible.

The effect of social science theorizing is not always to constrict the range of choice which official and other influential elites see as open to them. Thus, in his task of delimiting the possible the theorist may point to an expanded range of choice made possible by a more systematic exploitation of newly available means for achieving objectives. Modern mass media, for example, enable foreign relations to be conducted by communications addressed to opinion groups in foreign countries other than the government itself. Woodrow Wilson's appeal to the dissident nationalities of the old Austro-Hungarian Empire hastened the demise of that empire. In his time he was using an abnormal weapon, and using it to win a war. To make psychological strategy a "normal" adjunct of policy and thus to utilize modern mass media efficiently, whether in war or in peace, in the service of a nation's foreign policy, one has to have a theoretical model of world politics less simple than that of billiard balls of varying sizes, called "great powers" and "small powers," bouncing against each other on a green baize table called "power politics."

Without closely reasoned theories of international relations, social scientists can indeed render a disservice to foreign policymakers and other persons of influence by beckoning them up false paths, i.e., by seeming to make their range of choice greater or smaller than it really is. Slogans and clichés, and also the findings of modern social science which would work miracles if only the world would hold still long enough for the reform based on those findings to take effect, are no substitute for such theories. "Tensions breed war," but it by no means follows that every unilateral reduction in tension contributes to peace or to whatever values a government is trying to promote. Anything which relaxed tensions against Hitler in France, Britain and America during the 1930's, for example, contributed to making a big war inevitable, although it undoubtedly reduced the prospect of war at the moment.

For an analysis of the relation between tensions and war to be prescriptively useful, distinctions have to be developed. There is a difference between a selective relaxation of tension with respect to values that are not really threatened or are not really very valuable and a general relaxation which, if unilateral, might even be an invitation to aggression. There is a difference between demonstrating that an all-round reduction in tensions once achieved, would promote peace and security and showing, even if only in theory, how a staged reduction on a multilateral basis could provide a secure and peaceful transition to the new world of low-tension moral disarmament.

It would be easy to caricature and parody the prescriptions for saving the world which have from time to time been advanced by otherwise serious students of the social sciences whose views of world politics are uninformed by any tenable underlying theory. It would be easy; it would be amusing; but it might not be rewarding. The theorist then has his uses as a policeman to prevent other social scientists from crashing directly into the councils of high policy. He has a more positive function of orchestrating their insights into a symphony of understanding.[3]

The international relations theorist is, however, inadequately equipped for the task of providing a complete prescription for policy. He is likely to lack up-to-the-minute information, "contacts" to bring his information up to the minute, access to the final decision-maker, and skill in effective writing addressed to persons of lesser influence. If a first-class international relations scholar tries too hard to be *immediately* useful, he may only succeed in becoming a fourth-class journalist. He has a role as long as he acts as a social scientist. This social science role he abandons if he becomes a peddler of "current events" or an apologist for the reigning priests of high policy.

Theories are policy-relevant even in those cases in which the theories verge on the absurd. Thus, the spacists and the racists—with their theories whose empirical referents were shrouded in

[3] Cf. Kenneth N. Waltz, *Man, the State and War* (New York, 1959), ch. 3.

mystery and whose normative ambiguities made it impossible to disentangle their predictions and their preferences—were policy-relevant even though the purveyors of false theories. They are policy-relevant, whether they want to be or not, because their teaching and their preaching become part of the world political process on whose future they are supposed to be shedding light. The "decline of the West," for example, based on some belief that civilizations, like forms of higher life, pass through a natural life-cycle of birth, growth, maturity, decay and death, could be a self-confirming hypothesis to the extent that it promoted fatalism among those who under other circumstances might have thought the West had a future.

Similarly, some professional students of international relations in the United States in the 1920's tended to define the American choice in foreign policy as being between selfish isolationism and unselfish internationalism, between withdrawal from Europe and membership in the League of Nations. Those who might have chosen to support a policy based on the enlightened self-interest of continued American participation in maintaining the European order were not always provided with the theoretical basis for developing their position. Thus, in a negative way as well as in a positive way, international relations scholarship was policy-relevant even in the heyday of isolationism. It can lead or it can mislead, but it cannot help making a difference.

It is a short step to argue that if the theorist's work makes a difference willy-nilly, it behooves the international relations scholar to make sure that he is not accidentally affecting the future in ways he does not desire and that, within the limits of opportunity, he is affecting it in ways he regards as benign. To do this he may have to be somewhat more explicit in stating to himself and to his readers the basis for his selection of topics to investigate and the relevance of his conclusions to problems of public policy. Whether or not there is need for more theory, there is a need for theory to be more explicitly formulated.

II

The recent burst of activity which is unambiguously labelled "theoretical," might seem to imply that whatever intellectual activity was going on before, it was not sufficiently theoretical. What is this theory of international relations to which such frequent reference is being made? There is no body of propositions conventionally called "international relations theory" in the sense that there is "economic theory," nor is the history of international relations thought frequently taught under the course title, "international relations theory," the way the history of political thought is taught under the course title, "political theory." However, like the child who only discovers when he goes to school that he has been speaking English all the time, we students of international relations may discover that we have been theorizing all the time. None of us would have been willing in the pre-theory period to have our research described as "rootless empiricism," and what but some theory or other would have enabled us to avoid being written off as mere accumulators of facts? And how can what looks superficially like a jumble of data be ordered except by some theories of classification and interrelatedness? And how can we make statements about what our data "means" unless we have some theories as to what may be legitimately inferred from the data, and how these inferences may be related to other inferences based on other observations of the real world by other investigators?

On the other hand, let none of us fall into the opposite trap of ever imagining that what we are engaged in is pure theorizing. Try as we may to avoid it, and I for one hope we do not try very hard, there are always real or imagined empirical referents which a given theory allegedly illuminates.[4] It takes both carbon and oxygen, both digestion and respiration to maintain life. Similarly, it takes both "facts" and "theories" to achieve understanding of the world in which nations and states are born and die, compete and cooperate, live at war or at peace.

Theory is not an end in itself any more than data-collecting is an end in itself. The world in which we dwell does not exist simply to provide empirical verification for the plausibility of our theories. At the same time it cannot be understood by random, seriatim observations uninformed by any disciplined ordering of the observations.

[4] The distinction between "theory" and "research" which is here implied is not as black and white as the discussion suggests. An extremely general statement is incapable of direct empirical verification. An extremely specific statement is meaningless unless it is capable of such verification; but there is no clear line between "generality" and "specificity" of statement.

III

The recent rise in interest in both theory and doctrine [5] may be accounted for in a variety of ways: its narrow usefulness to the prestige-hungry scholar, its contribution to political science, and its hoped for contribution to wiser choices in public policy.

(1) The student of international relations is sensitive to the charge that he has no "theory" and has no history either. If he asserts that his analyses are policy-oriented, he may be told that pimping and pandering for the artificers of high policy in Washington or London or Moscow is not "scholarship" and in fact undermines objectivity. Stated bluntly, the international relations scholar would feel less inferior if he had a body of propositions as difficult for his colleagues to understand and evaluate as some of theirs are for him. Paradoxically, this stimulus to theorizing might make international relations studies less useful to the policy-maker; it would certainly make them less immediately useful.

(2) With the increasing emphasis in political science on the *process* of politics rather than simply on the *form* of institutions, the study of world politics as "politics in the absence of government," can be more easily understood as organically related to the classical study of political science. The fashion of referring to some or all of the social sciences as "behavioral sciences" or "policy sciences" has perhaps helped to focus interest on state behavior, on foreign policy, and on the processes of choice of decision-making elites.

(3) With the acceptance of the notion that somehow the world has changed, and world politics with it, in the era that has seen *inter alia* the passing of the European age, the rise of the superpowers, the Afro-Asian awakening, and the plural possession of thermonuclear weapons, the need is intensified for the observer to transcend his own time and culture and view them from some lofty point where the world politics of today can be seen as only one among a great variety of world political patterns that have been or

[5] It is desirable to distinguish between statements about what is, has been, might have been, will be, may be, or would be under specified conditions, and statements about what ought to be. Both types of propositions are included in the theoretical efforts described above, as indeed they are in the body of literature conventionally called "political theory." Lasswell and Kaplan call only the first "theory" and describe the propounding of norms as "doctrine" (H. D. Lasswell and A. Kaplan, *Power and Society* (New Haven, 1950). Cf. Mortimer Adler, *How to Think About War and Peace* (New York, 1944). Adler uses "theory" similarly but contrasts it with "practice" which, he says, involves the introduction of ethical considerations.

could be. Otherwise, one can hardly grasp the significantly novel and the significantly familiar aspects of contemporary world politics.

The first and no doubt healthy response to the recognition that the European state system had become a world system and that the United States as a world power had world-wide concerns was that non-Western European area studies needed encouragement, not only the Soviet Union, the Far East and Latin America but more recently Africa, the Middle East and the rest of the Asian rimlands. Thus, the effort to be liberated from European culture-bound perspectives is far advanced and largely successful. But understanding the whole of world politics is a greater task, or at any rate a different one, than understanding the sum of its parts; and it is widely believed that theory can help us comprehend the whole.

The new interest in theory may be partly due to wholly unwarranted expectations regarding the kind of theoretical and doctrinal guidance which the scholar can offer the statesman or the thoughtfully responsible citizen. Some of the reputation for being able to work magic which the physical scientists won for themselves at Hiroshima may have rubbed off on the social scientist. He may in some cases come to believe that he too is or could be a wonder-worker. With some of the old sign-posts gone and some of those that remain evidently pointing the wrong way, he may be tempted to believe that he has been "called" to point the way, to believe there is a one-to-one relationship between his theory and the "right" foreign policy for his country or for the world.

IV

Whatever may be the "use" of the study of international relations, by which I understand whatever may be its impact on world politics and particularly on the behavior of states, it is not to relate big theory directly to big policy. Speculative activity can be no more useful than the subject which it illuminates.[6]

Theorizing can define the principles of exclusion and inclusion so that the distinctive task of the international relations scholar is differentiated from the tasks of social scientists in general. It can define the changing task of the investigator as it is modified by gross changes in world politics and in the state of the art of the investigator. Thus, technological and scientific change, formerly viewed

[6] On the task of the theorist in the social sciences generally, see Robert K. Merton, *Social Theory and Social Structure* (Glencoe, Ill., 1949).

as a long-run variable, has in our generation come to be seen as a critical short-run variable; and technical possibilities for investigating the behavior of decision-making elites are making it possible to supplement traditional archival research with new methods for illuminating diplomatic behavior.

Theorizing also helps to define "important" subjects for investigation, i.e., important in terms of the investigators' value preferences. Arnold Wolfers' essay, "Political Theory and International Relations," has posed a very important question as to how much international relations thinking in Britain and America has been shaped by a philosophy of choice based on a real or imagined freedom of choice.[7] The present essay is perhaps an exemplification of such an attitude.

Theorizing ought to alert the investigator to limitations which are inherent in his mode of investigation. Is the baby being thrown out with the bath, for example, when one ignores the idiosyncratic behavior of individual states in order to discover certain laws about the behavior of states in general? How does one find a way of dealing with the unique as well as the recurring, of the particular as well as the general? Perhaps it depends on the question being asked, which of the two types of simplification of the real world is the more appropriate.

Any kind of rigor in scholarship requires that the ordering concepts be clarified. This theoretical activity has logically to precede data-collecting, although in actual research conceptual analysis is continually being stimulated by data which does not quite seem to fit. The verification or disverification of such a simple statement as that "All states seek to maximize their power positions" cannot proceed, for example, without defining and describing the "power" which is allegedly being maximized. Under one definition of power, the statement is hardly more than a tautology. Under another, power-seeking tends to be equated with all goal-oriented activity and thus may be that which differentiates animal from vegetable life, or at any rate, actions from thought. With conceptual analysis, the significant question might be transformed from whether or not states seek to maximize power to what kind of power what groups seek to maximize under what conditions.

"National character" is another frequently ambiguous ordering concept. Are we talking about some *Volksgeist* or an objectively

[7] A. Wolfers and L. Martin, eds., *The Anglo-American Traditions in Foreign Affairs* (New Haven, 1956), pp. ix-xvii.

verifiable regularity in mass behavior or attitude which distinguishes one national group (or its influential elites) from some or all others? [8]

When we refer to a state's "national interest" are we talking about something objectively definable or are we in some way referring to a policy which would be rational if one posited such and such a value position? [9] If one assumed with Charles Beard, for example, that United States foreign policy was an expression of the interest of the group which happened to have captured control of the national government, then one would be positing that there were no national goals to be served via foreign policy and that the idea of national interest was a fraud.[10] It is worth noting that Charles Beard did have strong views that Franklin D. Roosevelt's foreign policy was contrary to America's (non-existent) national interest.

The significant question and the ordering concept need to be supplemented by the working model. This is a crude (or refined) approximation of the real world simplified by the fact that it seeks to answer only certain questions by using only certain kinds of data. It is only useful as it helps us to answer the question we are asking. There is no reason to suppose any one model of world politics will be more generally useful than all others, or for that matter more general than all others. To be told that states make war upon each other because man is a power-seeking animal by no means explains why there is sometimes war and sometimes peace, nor does it tell us why certain combinations of states have fought or may fight certain others. A theoretical statement, to be useful, has to be discriminating. It has to be general enough to apply to classes of cases, but not so general as to have no empirical referents whatever.

The apparent chaos of interstate relations in a multiple-sovereignty system can be "ordered" in a variety of ways by disciplined and disinterested observers. Some observers see regularities in the behavior of the states they are observing which permit them to theorize about the behavior of states in general, e.g., "All states seek to maximize their power positions." Others are able to explain the cycles of victory and defeat which various states have experienced in terms of key relationships, e.g., that between the "haves"

[8] Cf. N. Leites, "Psycho-Cultural Hypotheses About Political Acts," *World Politics,* Vol. I, No. 1 (October 1948), pp. 102-119.

[9] See a symposium exchange of views, H. J. Morgenthau and W. T. R. Fox, "National Interest and Moral Principles in Foreign Policy" in *The American Scholar,* Vol. 18, No. 2 (Spring 1949), pp. 207-216.

[10] Cf. Charles A. Beard, *The Idea of National Interest* (New York, 1934).

and the "have nots" or that between "land power" and "sea power" or the struggle over some key area, the "Rimland," for example. Others leave questions of state motivation to one side and concern themselves solely with explanations for power differentials between states. No one of these approaches is more theoretical than another. None of them is necessarily incompatible with any other. What kind of abstraction is useful depends on the intellectual operation in which one is engaged.

Cartographers understand that no one flat map can be accurate as to more than one of the following: areas, directions, shapes. A globe sacrifices no two of these to the third, but it is incapable of showing detail and is of little use for navigation or geological surveys, for example. The analogy to international relations theory here suggested by cartography may be pertinent and exact.

No one theory may be equally accurate in explaining the cycle of peace and war, the rise and fall of great states, the extent to which the future is already implicit in the past, why certain states are "great powers," and so forth. A "global" theory which comprehended all these might not be of very much use in understanding, for example, how Western diplomacy has in our century sought to avoid having to deal with a Russo-German coalition. Theories of less architectonic proportions might be more useful in explaining this particular uniformity of state behavior, although of little use in some other context.

A theory which explains why States A, B, C. . . . are strong and J, K, L. . . . are not has its role, particularly if strength and/or weakness is really explained. While useful, it would have the same limited usefulness as the anthropologist's conception of a "pecking order" in indigenous cultures. It explains who has what—e.g., "status is measured by the number of cattle one owns"—but not who gets what, i.e., what qualities cause one's herd of cattle to grow and his fellow's to shrink. A conception of a pecking order in our state system is useful if one is seeking to explain the behavior of states in a state system at any given time or within a time period too short for the pecking order to be modified. It is useless to explain why the family of great powers changes, sometimes even without inter-great-power war. It is equally useless in explaining how a policy-maker can achieve for his state optimum security in an insecure world or how states generally can achieve an all-around increase in security.

It is idle to ask which model is best. Models, like concepts, need to be operationally defined and this depends on the prior identification of the significant operation—here again, "prior" in logic though not necessarily in time. A model which helped to make plausible the passing of the European age—as did, for example, Harold Sprout's analysis of the political consequences of nineteenth-century and twentieth-century improvements in overland transport [11]—might not be very useful in defining the conditions under which the super-powers could be expected to agree to arms limitation agreements in the field of manufacture, stockpiling, or delivery of nuclear weapons.

To be efficient, we have said, theories of international relations are necessarily partial; they are not equally useful for the answer of all questions. If only because they are partial, because they are only true *ceteris paribus,* one should hesitate before vaulting directly from theory to policy prescription. The greater the awareness and the more explicit the definition of "the other things being equal" qualification, the more efficient international relations theory can be in serving posited value positions, i.e., the more useful it can be as a rational guide to policy.

The study of international relationships may possibly, like modern physics, evolve toward the discovery of some inherent relationship among its ordering concepts of such elegant simplicity as Einstein's statement that energy is equal to mass multiplied by the square of the speed of light. But whether or not the student of international relations will ever attain a comparable level of general theoretical insight, he is not likely to be able to leap to that level of insight simply by closing the door of his study and speculating about power, the national interest, and the state of nature in world politics. And if, by any chance, a theorist today should stumble upon some simple, central truth about world politics which seems to explain a wide array of the phenomena of international politics, the chance is slight that he would be able to get general acceptance of either the correctness or the importance of the revolutionary new theoretical insight.

In the meantime, let us be tolerant, even if sometimes skeptical, of each other's theories; as Mao Tse-tung has said, but apparently no longer believes: "Let all flowers bloom." We shall probably find it easier to agree that some of these flowers are weeds than that any one of the others is the fairest flower of all.

---

[11] H. and M. Sprout, *Foundations of National Power* (Princeton, 1945).

How shall we distinguish the weeds from the flowers? Let us call "weeds": (1) those theoretical statements that do not purport to answer questions we regard as important or relevant; (2) those whose ordering concepts have no clear empirical referents or ones so ambiguous that they are incapable of verification or disverification, much less proof; (3) those which create a model of world politics which is such a distortion of reality that it obfuscates rather than clarifies when one tries to relate the imagined world to the observed one; (4) those that fail to take account of variables important to the answering of the question being asked; (5) those with more variables than are essential to give an equally accurate answer; (6) those that turn out on analysis to be tautological; (7) those that conceal within themselves assumptions of which their author is not fully aware; (8) those that are parochial because their author has presented them as transcendent but has failed to transcend his own time, or class, or ethnic affiliation; (9) those that are internally inconsistent; (10) those with unambiguous empirical referents whose behavior is inconsistent with the theory; (11) those that confuse statements of fact and of preference; (12) those which are *post factum* and topical; (13) those that prescribe for the world as if it were a clean slate on which anything could be written.[12]

V

The relationship between theory and policy is two-way, complex and sometimes indirect. One of the reasons, we have said, why a given problem may be regarded as "significant" or worth working on is that its solution is regarded as important to promoting or maintaining certain values. But the significant problem may seem to defy solution if attacked directly. Intensive search for the cure for the war disease may take place quite far from the site of the war epidemic, and this in turn may beckon the investigator on to new explorations whose relation to the original problem is only dimly perceived if it is even considered at all. It may often happen

[12] Weeds in the flower garden of theory are often found where the earth is richest, and what is one man's flower may be another man's weed. J. U. Nef, *War and Human Progress* (Cambridge, Mass., 1950), is a work of first-rate importance for anyone speculating about technology and international relations, although the question the author seeks to answer, "Does war contribute to human progress?" is not one which an international relations theorist would be likely to ask; nor is Professor Nef's answer one which is of either descriptive or prescriptive significance with respect to the decisions of leaders of national governments to embark upon or refrain from embarking upon particular wars.

that the solution to a problem comes while one is working on quite a different problem. But without a theoretical framework one might miss the key insight which one "accidentally" discovers.

For the relationship of theory to policy to be one-way, simple and direct, several conditions would have to be met. Theory would have to be a pyramidal, symmetrical structure of ideas whose highest point encompassed all the wisdom of the lower levels. The theorist and the policy-makers would have to be in perfect understanding as to the values being promoted. Finally, the theory would have to provide the discriminating basis for choice among all policy alternatives, major and minor, without the addition of either further theories or further facts.

With or without a theory of international relations, the findings of modern social science will be utilized in an era of efficient public administration and protracted high-level mobilization in much the same way that any other community resource will be utilized. If sociologists can demonstrate how friction can be alleviated between personnel in large military installations and the population of neighboring cities, they may make members of the armed forces abroad more efficient instruments of national policy. If social psychologists can illuminate the theory of small-group behavior, there may be some useful clues as to how American negotiators ought to behave in specified international conference situations. This *ad hoc* utilization for the more efficient conduct of foreign relations of this or that research finding differs, however, in no important respect from the way in which any large-scale enterprise, private or public, would utilize it. There is no theoretical problem raised by the addition of such insights on a piecemeal basis to the intellectual capital of the student of world politics or the practitioner of diplomacy.

One can therefore eliminate in advance one type of question from the agenda of theory, viz.: "What is the nature of the general contribution to international relations which sociology (or psychology or anthropology or statistics or geography or history or what have you) makes?" The answer is that sociology (psychology, etc.) in general, does not contribute to international relations in general. Specific sociological (psychological, etc.) insights may provide practical and sometimes direct assistance to the policy-maker. They also become, like other records of human action, data of possible relevance to the international relations theorist. No overarching theory is, however, required for a diplomatist to make use of a report that in certain cultures it is conventional to grin when reporting a personal tragedy; and it is difficult to see how such a report would be of any direct use to the theorist, however helpful it might be to a diplomat on a specific occasion.

Let us consider, however, some other contributions of the non-political sciences. The accumulation of evidence that differences in skin pigmentation and all other physical differences which are conventionally associated with "race" correlate in no significant way with innate intellectual capacity, has evidently had a powerful effect on theories of international relations which presupposed permanently unequal relations between political groupings of Western European culture and what were widely believed to be lesser breeds in God's scheme of things. The accumulating evidence that man typically strives to maximize a multiplicity of values serves to warn those who may create theoretical models based on some simplistic assumption that men or groups of men subordinate their every action to the maximization of some one value—material gain, power, self-respect, etc.[13] Theorists, in general, and single-value systematizers in particular, may not legitimately prescribe for the ills of the real world without taking full account of the simplifications which, knowingly or unknowingly, they introduce into their theoretical model. Social science can be a corrective both to Marx and to Machiavelli, as well as to those who would follow them in too slavish a fashion.

The data on race and on value-maximization have something in common which distinguishes them from the earlier cited examples of the direct *ad hoc* application of one particular finding of social science to one particular form of social action—the conduct of foreign relations. Their impact on foreign policy and on world politics generally is indirect. In each case the new data has affected scholars' images of world politics. These modifications in theoretical perspective in time are diffused "up" to policy-making levels which are more immediately influential.

This type of contribution to the continuing reconstruction of the scholar's image of world politics can be made on the initiative of the scholar himself, provided he has the curiosity to keep abreast of advances in the behavioral sciences and to ask questions of his non-international relations colleagues which he alone can ask and they alone can answer. It can also be made on the initiative of the

[13] See H. D. Lasswell, "The Normative Impact of the Behavioral Sciences," *Ethics*, Vol. LXVII, No. 3 (April 1957), Part II.

non-international relations behavioral scientist, provided his knowledge of the matrix of thinking about world politics is sufficient to enable him to know what kinds of questions the international relations scholar would ask if he knew the data existed, or could be made to exist, to answer those questions.

This is the kind of contribution which can lead to complications and refinements of the theoretician's model of world politics. The complexity however may become so great that the model comes to resemble a Rube Goldberg apparatus. The intellectual output may be somewhat less than its input unless there is selective simplification of the model in the light of both the question being asked and the latest relevant findings of the behavioral sciences.

Simplification may sometimes flow from ignorance and even from a willful determination to ignore inconvenient data, but a scholar's simplification is deliberate. Suppose it is true that power is sought most frequently as a means of achieving non-power ends, but suppose it generally turns out, within the context of the international relations question being investigated, that power is regarded as the sole reliable means to achieve the other "higher" (i.e., more socially acceptable) ends. Note, however, the qualification, "suppose it generally turns out. . . ." If research should show, for example, that it was something called "security" rather than something called "power" towards which at least some states moved, say the rich and fat ones, or the insular ones, or those which could have no real hope of ever being top rooster in the international pecking order, the model might have to be modified. Or suppose analysis should show that all the hard choices which a government had to make in foreign and military policy related not to the question whether to seek power but rather to the question: "What kind and how much shall we mobilize to meet which combination of threats during what time periods?" Then the model, at least for short-term analysis, would have to be reconsidered.

In the absence of data, a theoretical model tends to be simple. New data must, initially at least, complicate the model, although as relationships become clearer and correlations closer the number of genuinely independent variables to be handled may ultimately decrease.

More typically, we have said, models are simplified "operationally." If one's concern is to establish the limits within which the family of great powers is to be expected to vary over the next half century—this would have been a very useful exercise a century or so ago, and De Tocqueville and List did predict the emergence of the great Russian and American super-powers—one can immediately exclude all kinds of data relevant to the answer of other equally important international relations questions. To summarize, ignorant and unintended simplifications of reality reduce the relevance of theory to policy, while operational simplifications enhance its relevance.

Theory operates, however indirectly, to modify the attitudes and beliefs both of a government's supporters and of its potential effective critics. In both cases, greater theoretical insight acts to increase the rationality of choice of the policy-maker. Through theoretical investigations certain goals are seen to be unreal or unattainable or inconsistent with other "higher" goals or more costly than previously imagined. Other goals may come to be seen as more possible than was once generally believed. Thus, the theorist not only heightens the rationality of the decision-maker's choices, but he provides the decision-maker with the basis for reformulating his value position.

VI

The future is not a *tabula rasa* on which we are free to write what we choose. But neither are we puppets dancing on the stage of history in response to "first causes," "basic factors," or, for that matter, inevitable progress toward bringing the Kingdom of God down on this earth. Rational political action consists in achieving the best possible reconciliation of the desirable and the possible.

We ought therefore to attempt to order the blooming, buzzing confusion of world politics by collecting and arranging our data so that it helps us to understand the relatively fixed, the changing but uncontrollable, and manipulatable aspects of world politics. Within the range of the changeable, we need to collect data which help us to predict ever more accurately the consequences of particular courses of action.

If man is to have the opportunity to exercise some measure of rational control over his destiny, the limits of the possible and the consequences of the desirable have both to be investigated. A theory of international relations is thus needed which distinguishes:

a) the "givens" in the world political equation—*e.g.*, resources, shapes of continents, conception of politics as an unending process (however its form may change);

b) long-run basic changes—*e.g.*, rise of nationalism, spread of coal-and-iron technology, the demographic revolution;
c) the policies of other states over which one's own state has relatively slight control and the policies of one's own state which are not chosen primarily in a foreign policy context;
d) the remaining area of choice—*e.g.*, levels of preparedness; patterns of alliance; use of organization to adjust conflict or facilitate peaceful change.

Whether one views world politics from the desk of a great-power foreign minister at a critical moment of choice or from the desk of a scholar in a university during an inter-crisis period of peace, there must almost inevitably be a restless search for the variables in the situation which one can modify and which, if modified, would result in a more efficient protection or promotion of whatever the viewer, whether policy-maker or theorist, regards as valuable. Each seeks to bring about a reconciliation of the desirable and the possible along lines more satisfactory than had hitherto seemed feasible to him.

Not all of the factors which the theorist must in proper humility— writing away from the seat of government, outside the domain of official secrecy and before the event—label as an area of choice, will be seen as such by the man on the inside at the moment of choice. The maker of policy also lacks perfect knowledge, however much his areas of ignorance may have been narrowed by general theoretical understanding or specific official intelligence. His choices lack the clarity which historians and social scientists, after the event and with their bias toward orderly explanations, impose on his action. But it is his sense of the deficiency of the theoretical and practical guidance available to him at moments of difficult choice which is one source in the formulation of new "problems" and the restarting of the policy-theory-policy cycle of interaction.

The theorist's quest for precise definition and imaginative expansion of the range of future choice should lead him to focus neither on the absolutely invariant nor on the inherently unknowable or the completely uncontrollable. The realms of the wholly fixed or wholly predictable and the wholly uncontrollable need to be defined, but the energies of research and theory ought to concentrate on that which lies in between.

The shape of the continents is fixed and so is the distribution of natural resources under the earth's crust. The atom has been split and nuclear weapons can hardly be "un-invented," except under circumstances that would make theorizing about future politics irrelevant.

Population growth rates are changing and changing at different rates. Whether or not governments can significantly affect differentials in growth rates, they are hardly likely to do so in a foreign policy context. Here too is a type of "given" which has to be set down and kept in mind, a dynamic factor which cannot be manipulated either in the Foreign Office or in the study of the international relations scholar.

Ideas and attitudes are perhaps more subject to deliberate modification, although the scholar and the artificer of foreign policy have no long-run monopoly in manipulating thought and not much possibility of significantly influencing it at all in the short-run.[14] Nationalism as a force runs deep, and its recent development in Africa and Asia could probably not have been thwarted by any policy whatever. Its impact on policy in Europe and North America, however, can surely be modified by theoretical discussion of the North Atlantic community, of Western European integration, and of Western relations with the ex-colonial areas.

The United States government cannot by any particular foreign policy relieve the population pressure in India or raise Chinese living standards to equal American standards. But if it has greater understanding than it now does of the specific political consequences of various forms of military, economic and technical assistance and of alternative psychological strategies, it can minimize some of the undesired consequences of the prevailing inequality in living standards.

United States diplomacy cannot by applying what is known about the behavior of diplomatists within the Western European culture area operate with maximum efficiency in other culture areas, but the promotion of area studies can help close this particular gap.

Wishing will not make super-powers of the former European great powers; but an analysis of the political consequences of varying degrees of West European integration reveals, as an ultimate possibility, the creation of a single West European super-power. It thus clarifies discussion in a genuine area of choice.

Analysis of the changed significance of power potential in an era in which a new world war might be very short, can highlight the

---

[14] In the short run a selective presentation of "facts" can, of course, gain for the policy-maker some immediate freedom of maneuver.

critical nature of government decisions regarding the defense budget.

Neither side can compel arms limitation agreements, but the conditions under which restrictions on nuclear arms would make both sides feel more secure can be clarified by stating the problem with theoretical rigor.

The former colonial and semi-colonial populations can hardly be made to love those whom they only recently regarded as exploiters, but this does not mean that the actions of Western states make no difference or that one course of action will not serve a given value position much better than another.

In a longer time perspective, it may be that some of the features of our state system which have been regarded as invariant—the balance of power and national self-determination as both expectations and norms; total war as a feasible policy alternative, etc.—may turn out to be characteristic only of our state system in a particular stage of its evolution. What are the range of alternative futures which the theorist can envision? These must be systematically described before those in and out of government whose opinions determine policy can rationally select policy.

The key words in this analysis have been "theory," "doctrine," and "policy." Theory is useful because it organizes social science so as, marginally at least, to heighten the rationality of choice, official and unofficial. It does not do this directly; it does it by clarifying doctrinal positions, by pointing to the most efficient means to move toward desired ends, and by minimizing the area of contingency and sheer ignorance which the policy-maker can never hope completely to eliminate. More specifically, theory can focus research on what might be called the quasi-contingent, the factors that are neither absolutely invariant or uncontrollable nor absolutely unknown or unpredictable.

VII

The vocation of leadership is a stern one, and a scholar is not solely by virtue of his scholarly attributes equipped to lead. Politics, as Max Weber wrote in another time of trouble, "is the strong and slow boring of hard boards." This observation applies also to international politics. The moral imperative is no less, it is indeed greater, and the task is arduous. The social scientist must be aware both of his potentialities and his limitations *as a social scientist* if he is to perform his distinctive function, but he need be no moral eunuch to perform that function. He must never forget that as a social scientist he is not called upon to tell men what they ought to want. If international politics is the slow boring of hard boards, it is not the social scientist's task either to assert that the boards are in fact soft or to say where the holes ought to be bored. It is his task to say where the knots are likely to be if he knows, and what consequences may properly be expected if boring takes place here rather than there, and to provide as sharp tools as possible for the boring. To perform this task he needs to construct a frame in which systematic and imaginative hypothesizing most readily occurs. In other words, he must make use of theory.

VI

GROWING POINTS IN THE STUDY OF INTERNATIONAL RELATIONS*

Approaches to the study of international relations have in the first two-thirds of the twentieth century generally been cumulative. International law and diplomatic history were already well-established by 1900. The inter-war period saw international government and various "devil" theories of international relations—with munitions-makers, imperalists and capitalists variously cast as devils—flourish. By the beginning of World War II realist schools stressing the power drives of men and states were well-established, and geographical influences on world political patterns were the object of attention. Tensions as causes of war, the behavior of decision-making elites, national security policy, conflict resolution, systems and their transformations have all been foci of interest in post-World War II international relations research. Although some of the devil theories and the pseudo-science of geopolitics today seem dated, the newer types of international relations research have in each period ordinarily complemented but not displaced the older. Ours is an expanding and not merely a changing subject.

The growth of arcane literature and proliferation of infelicitous neologisms has wrung from the layman the kind of respect he gives to men with a terminology he cannot understand. Graduate stu-

* Prepared for the dedication program of the Von KleinSmid Center of International and Public Affairs, University of Southern California, October 1, 1966.

dents in political science have turned in increasing numbers to international and comparative studies; and in one large university (Columbia) three-quarters of the doctoral dissertations in political science were written in these fields in the 1960-65 period. The "Charles River Complex" of Harvard University and Massachusetts Institute of Technology scholars in international affairs contributed a generous share of cortical cells to the Kennedy Administration's foreign policy brain. An International Studies Association with its own journal, *International Studies Quarterly,* has been established.[1] Academic consultants on foreign and military affairs flow into Washington, and academic research contracts flow out.

Such evidence of new affluence and prestige are, however, at least partly misleading. Neither generous funding nor lay deference measures intellectual progress. Even if either did, the case for progress in international relations research would still not be made; for the "international, comparative and regional studies" which have commanded so much financial support are far broader in scope than the academic study of international relations. "International relations" (or "international politics" or "world politics"), I believe, ought to be the matrix subject into which other international, comparative and regional studies are fitted. So defined, it is proper that "international relations" consume only a modest fraction of the resources available for all international studies. The study of exotic areas is necessarily costly, and he who would measure the progress and locate the growing points of international relations research must look elsewhere than to the university's cash box.

The stimuli to increased study of international relations are many. Changes in the world political environment and tools of analysis developed by other branches of learning, as well as the normal evolution of a subject by able and dedicated scholars working in the field and the generous support of the foundations, are hastening the pace of development. Thus, developments in natural science have changed both the world political environment and the means for studying that environment. It is enough to mention the nuclear-electronic revolution in military technology to illustrate the former; the computer revolution in information storage, retrieval and analysis illustrates the latter.

Perhaps because international relations has become too serious a business to be left in the hands of international relations scholars, "social psychologists, political sociologists, mathematical biologists,

[1] Until 1966, this journal was called *Background.*

nuclear physicists and disillusioned theologians"—to use Ernst Haas' listing, and he might have added economists—have, sometimes but by no means always under the banner of "peace research," all contributed in the past decade to constructing models for an allegedly more scientific study of the subject.[2] Since 1957, when it began publication, the *Journal of Conflict Resolution* has been a main conduit for pouring this new literature into the stream of international relations and thinking.[3]

The methods and models of economists and mathematicians have made game theory, theories of bilateral monopoly and conflict resolution, and cost-benefit analysis relevant both to the academic study of international relations and to the decision processes of responsible officials. Systems theorists have sought to make the self-maintaining and self-modifying aspects of our contemporary state systems understandable in ways not possible through more familiar techniques of balance-of-power analysis.

The work of Charles A. W. Manning merits separate mention. His *The Nature of International Society*[4] is a kind of systems-building effort to describe "a social cosmos" which derives from philosophical sociology. It is almost accidental that Professor Manning's book first appeared in the 1960s; for it is the careful expression of a sustained and slowly-matured point of view familiar to a generation of his students and by hearsay or in fragmentary fashion to his professional colleagues. In this "pre-scientific" phase of the study of international relations—using "pre-scientific" in Thomas Kuhn's sense—many paradigms for the study of international relations clamor for attention.[5] The Manning paradigm, which demonstrates at every point the author's insistently reiterated belief in the separateness of the discipline of international relations, is one with which the profession will have to come to terms; but because of its independent development the evaluation may come at as deliberate a pace as its formulation.

---

[2] *Beyond the Nation-State* (Stanford, Calif.: Stanford University Press, 1964), p. 51. A mathematical biologist's contribution is Anatol Rapoport, *Fights, Games and Debates* (Ann Arbor: University of Michigan Press, 1960). An economist's is Kenneth E. Boulding, *Conflict and Defense: A General Theory* (New York: Harper and Row, 1962).

[3] For example, it published a symposium issued on the work of the late British Quaker physicist, Lewis F. Richardson, whose *Arms Races and Insecurity* and *Statistics of Deadly Quarrels* (Chicago: Quadrangle Books, 1960) were posthumously published.

[4] London: G. Bell and Sons, Ltd., 1962.

[5] Thomas S. Kuhn, *The Structure of Scientific Revolutions* (Chicago: University of Chicago Press, 1962).

I do not choose to call our subject, in its present state, a discipline. It has neither a distinctive method of analysis nor an agreed paradigm for investigation to give it unity. It is, as Frederick S. Dunn said in the 1940s, a field defined by its problems rather than by its methods, "politics in the absence of central authority." The expectation of violence, to use Harold Lasswell's phrase, underlies every political calculation. The methods of international relations research are as varied as ever. There is no single frontier on which all the best minds or advanced students are working; and I cannot therefore make any straight-line projection of the next decade's developments in our field.

The powerful impact of scholars as diverse as Harold Lasswell, Karl Deutsch and Morton Kaplan has depended in the case of each on their making relevant to the study of international relations unorthodox skills of analysis. Charles McClelland has turned to general systems theory and Ernst Haas to functional sociology for their paradigms. Herman Kahn, Thomas Schelling and Albert Wohlstetter are (or were) "outsiders" who have come to occupy central positions in the development of the study of international relations. The inherent interest of our field is impressively demonstrated by the wide variety of skills laid on the altar of international relations research.[6] There is no sign that the "insiders" have either the wish or the possibility of barring the gate to these friendly interlopers.

Science for science's sake and theory for theory's sake students of international relations may deplore the fact, but it is the widespread belief that better understanding of the international system will lead to better policies by the actors in that system that accounts for whatever affluence and prestige international relations scholars now enjoy. War, particularly two-way thermonuclear war, is for us what cancer is for medical research.

More peace and security for more people more of the time, like better health more of the time for more people, are goals which command support for research. The analogy to medical research must not, however, be pushed too far. It is not "disease" but cancer or some other specific morbid condition that the medical researcher studies, even though "disease" is what gives unity to the totality of medical research. "War," and the even more general

[6] Quincy Wright's *Study of International Relations* (New York: Appleton-Century-Crofts, 1955) remains after a decade the most comprehensive and systematic inventory of the theoretical and practical disciplines which shape the contemporary study of the subject.

term, "conflict," like "disease," may be unifying symbols for international relations research; but they are too coarse concepts for manageable, detailed research. Peace can be broken and security threatened in a myriad of ways that do not yield to generalized prescription.[7] However, just as fundamental theoretical research on life processes may be financed by a society bent on finding a cure for cancer, students of international relations may spend some of their energies building the theoretical foundations for a later, more sophisticated direct assault on problems of war and peace.[8] Who knows when a tree in the orchard of international relations theory and research will grow an apple to drop on the head of a passing international relations Newton? It is a prudent investment for our society to subsidize the investigator of exotic far-out ideas as willingly as it subsidizes the investigator of exotic far-off places.

"Practical" men with funds to allocate for research on peace and security and "theoretical" men with intellectual curiosities to satisfy about our multiple-sovereignty system usually find it possible to deal frankly with each other, even if in extreme cases the researcher interprets his research mandate broadly or tailors his grant request slavishly to what he thinks are the grantor's predispositions. Programmed and unprogrammed research alike, theoretical as well as applied, reflect the dramatic changes in world politics in our generation and the moral concerns about these changes which the professional student translates into problems for scientific investigation.

The "real" world of international politics has taxed the ingenuities of the scientific observer whether or not he has a propensity to be socially useful.[9] The apparent poverty of power based upon

---

[7] This was a main conclusion of Quincy Wright's *Study of War* (Chicago: University of Chicago Press, 1942).

[8] See Harold D. Lasswell, *The Future of Political Science* (New York: Atherton Press, 1963), for the cancer metaphor and for an assertion of the need of social scientists to be as self-confident as natural scientists in budgeting for the unforseen hunch. For them, too, as Alvin M. Weinberg has suggested in justifying the support of "pure" natural science, non-policy-oriented international relations research may be regarded as "a necessary overhead or social capital cost." See Bruce L. R. Smith, "The Concept of Scientific Choice," *American Behavioral Scientist*, May 1966, p. 28.

[9] In a discussion of the uses of the computer and simulation in international relations research, a skeptic recalled how they weighed pigs in his native East Tennessee. (The discussion occurred at a panel session of the 1965 annual meeting of the American Political Science Association.) The pigs were put on one end of a teeter-totter, rocks were put on the other, and then the men sat around and guessed how much the rocks weighed. Are not all students of international relations today in a position a little like that of the pig-weigher? The pigs of the real world of international politics and the rocks of the observed world of the scientific international relations researcher are somehow related; but until we know how much the rocks weigh, we cannot be quite sure what

thermonuclear striking capacity in the era of the balance of terror has forced the growth of strategic studies of "lesser" instruments of violence and limited forms of interstate competition. Hesitant steps toward unity in Western Europe, giant steps toward balkanization of much of the rest of the world, and polycentrist tendencies on both sides of the Iron Curtain have generated a new interest in studies of integration, federation, alliances, disintegration, nationalism and political development. Thus, the scholar's perception of events which constitute for him "world politics" have a feed-back effect, for they alter what events he looks for and how he goes about looking for them.

The subject of international relations has had, however, a momentum of development of its own. The growth of interest, for example, in non-normative theory and new kinds of data-collecting is impressive.[10] Whether or not those engaged in such speculation and investigations believe their activities to be ultimately useful, their concern for immediate policy relevance is often minimal. Without reference either to the innovating stimuli or to the motivations of the researcher—for intellectual curiosity and an aspiration to be policy-relevant are equally compatible with canons of scientific rigor and are not mutually exclusive—several growing points in the study of international relations may be identified under five somewhat overlapping headings: concept formation, data acquisition, systems analysis, new actors, and the decision process.

Power and Restraint

Definition of the allegedly focal concept of power, in international relations as well as in political science generally, continues to be elusive. Earlier studies of "power factors" left unexplicated how the factors were to be combined but generally carried the implication that a power index could be computed for each state

---

we have learned about the real world that we originally set out to investigate. Two observers, Harold Guetzkow and Lloyd Jensen, finesse the problem of relating the "real" and the "observed" worlds, the pigs and the rocks in the metaphor, by speaking of "the so-called 'real world' " ("Research Activities on Simulated International Processes," *Background,* Feb. 1966, p. 269).

[10] Studies prepared for the most recent "self-survey" committee support this statement. This is a committee on research evaluation organized in 1964 by the Carnegie Endowment for International Peace with Philip E. Mosely as chairman and Hayward R. Alker, Jr., as rapporteur. E. Raymond Platig was the staff associate for the Endowment in the Committee and an active participant. See also Charles A. McClelland, *Theory and the International System* (New York: Macmillan, 1966).

actor in our state system. One cannot in fact add so many units of population, so many units of industrial production and so many units of will to sacrifice to so many units of advantageous geographic location and get any meaningful answer.[11] Even when the difficulty of combining power factors has been recognized, country-by-country power studies make sense only on the assumption that power is a discoverable essence. The power as essence concept was implicit in the very title and organization of Harold and Margaret Sprout's *Foundations of National Power*[12] published in the earlier post-war years. It is significant that in their successor volume, *Foundations of International Politics*,[13] they explicitly refer to the growing (but by no means novel) tendency to define power as a relationship rather than as an essence. Their own use of the term "political potentials" seems to stress the relativity of power (whatever it is) to the conflicting purposes of the actor and the acted upon. The evident intractability of "weak" states in the post-imperial age has posed questions about the bargaining base of the lesser power on issues of vital concern which lead to a clearer understanding of the range of choice of both great powers and small powers. On the other hand, the ineffectiveness of even "strong" states with unresolved domestic conflict (and the consequent "privatization" of their behavior when seen in the context of world politics) is plain to see. Thus, contemporary students of power recognize the relativity of power of a particular state to its goals and to the goals and capabilities of competitors, as well as the non-additivity of power factors.[14]

Karl Deutsch in his *Nerves of Government*[15] moves the concept of power from the center of the political science stage. In his cybernetic approach to both international and domestic politics, an actor's power consists in not having to adapt and perhaps in not even having to think.[16] It consists in getting those acted upon to do

---

[11] See, however, F. Clifford German, "A Tentative Evaluation of World Power," *Journal of Conflict Resolution*, March, 1960, pp. 138-44, in which the author seems to have worked backward from a common-sense power ranking of contemporary states toward the elaboration of power indices which when combined would ratify common sense.

[12] Princeton, N. J.: Princeton University Press, 1945; revised edition, New York: D. Van Nostrand, 1952.

[13] New York: D. Van Nostrand, 1962.

[14] On non-additivity in quantified research on world politics generally, see Hayward R. Alker, Jr., "The Long Road to International Relations Theory: Problems of Statistical Nonadditivity," *World Politics*, July, 1966, pp. 623-55.

[15] New York: Free Press of Glencoe, 1963.

[16] General Whitehead came close to saying the same thing: "Wars are won with power, not brains."

whatever adapting is thereby made necessary.[17] It follows that what is critical to the study of world politics is the flow of communications among the actors and the consequent learning process by which each overcomes or adapts to restraints which the system has signalled. This is fair enough if the bits of metal exchanged through the air by modern states in wartime are also treated as messages.

Charles J. Hitch and Roland M. McKean in their pioneering *Economics of Defense in the Nuclear Age*[18] arrive at very nearly the same point, although by a different route. They turn the whole power problem upside down and ask not what is the power of a given actor in a system but what factors operate to prevent the attainment of specified objectives. Restraint-analysis thus appears policy-relevant because it eliminates the intellectual waste motion of assaying the actor's capacity to do that which it has evinced no interest in doing.[19]

The Computer, the Scenario and the Case

The past decade in international relations research has seen a revolution in the kinds of data assembled for analysis. New concepts, new approaches, new hypotheses and new hunches point the way to the assembling of new data, and the data in turn may yield new hypotheses. The act of creating a general data bank poses questions of inclusion, exclusion and comparability of data.[20] The programming of computers able to manipulate the data also poses questions of the scope and method of international relations whose answers may be important to the subject's development.

---

[17] Deutsch discussed a not entirely dissimilar effort of Robert A. Dahl to define power in probabilistic terms, the probability that A will cause B to modify his behavior with respect to A's objective (*ibid.*, pp. 113-16).

[18] Cambridge, Mass.: Harvard University Press, 1960.

[19] Inis Claude in his *Power and International Relations* (New York: Random House, 1962) appears to be concerned with helping today's first-ranking states achieve self-restraint with respect to the power which at least two now have to achieve effects which none of them apparently wants. In this one respect, defining the term "power" to include the capacity to achieve unintended consequences, Claude resembles E. H. Carr in the latter's *Twenty Years' Crisis* (London: Macmillan, 1939). On Claude's analysis of "the management of power," see my review in *Journal of Conflict Resolution*, September, 1964, pp. 297-300.

[20] See Lasswell, *The Future of Political Science*, for a discussion of the need and specifications for a "basic data survey." Although Professor Lasswell describes the collection and provisional classification of available information as "Step One," he is already taking the first step when he specifies what to collect.

Content analyses have grown in number and sophistication. Karl Deutsch has stimulated the collection of data on the flow of international communications. The more systematic study of comparative politics has generated a need for "cross-polity" surveys[21] and handbooks of comparative political and social data.[22] The computer revolution has created a new technology in international relations research as in other areas of social science, and new methods of storing and retrieving data are opening the way for new kinds of quantitative analysis.[23] The flood of data will no doubt create as many problems as it solves.

Data for the study of world politics need not always be "gathered." It can also be invented. The computer makes it possible for a fantastic variety of imagined data to be subjected to systematic analysis. Simulation, so important in operations research, has become available as a tool for the study of "inter-nation" relations.[24] Where diplomatic history is inadequate for providing suggestive analogies, alternate scenarios can be written for the future. Here a sharpened pencil rather than a computer may turn out to be the most important research tool. Crises can be war gamed, and data thus accumulated and analyzed of a history that has never (yet, at least) occurred.[25]

"Decisions" and "crises" have provided widely discussed rubrics for data classification and collection. Richard C. Snyder at Northwestern University (now at the University of California at Irvine) and Robert C. North at Stanford University have applied intensively their schemes for data collecting and analysis of decisions and crises to the case of the American decision to intervene in the Korean War and to the crisis of July 1914, respectively. These are

[21] Arthur S. Banks and Robert Textor, *A Cross-Polity Survey* (Cambridge, Mass.: M.I.T. Press, 1963). See also Richard L. Merritt and Stein Rokkan, eds., *Comparing Nations: The Use of Quantitative Data in Cross-National Comparisons* (New Haven: Yale University Press, 1966).

[22] Bruce M. Russett, Hayward R. Alker, Jr., Karl W. Deutsch and Harold Lasswell, *World Handbook of Political and Social Indicators* (New Haven: Yale University Press, 1964). Norton Ginsberg, *Atlas of Economic Development* (Chicago: University of Chicago Press, 1961), has assembled a variety of comparative data useful to the student of world politics though with less explicitly political criteria of inclusion and exclusion.

[23] See Alker and Russett, *World Politics in the General Assembly* (New Haven: Yale University, 1965); Russett, *Community and Contention* (Cambridge, Mass.: M.I.T. Press, 1963); and Russett, *Trends in World Politics* (New York: Macmillan, 1965). More generally, see Alker, *Mathematics and Politics* (New York: Macmillan, 1965).

[24] Guetzkow *et al., Simulation in International Relations* (Englewood Cliffs, N. J.: Prentice-Hall, 1963).

[25] The Rand Corporation and its East Coast private enterprise offshoot, the Hudson Institute under Herman Kahn's leadership, have provided environments favorable to inventors of this kind of data.

not the only examples of the intensive study of élite behavior, as we shall see in our later discussion of research on the decision process. It may be premature to speculate what kinds of "cross-decision" and "cross-crisis" surveys (to match the "cross-polity" surveys) will be possible when many cases and crises have been studied in comparable detail, and even more premature to speculate what kind of analysis of world politics would then become possible.

The System and Its Transformation

In 1949 I described a post-World War II shift in the dominant scholarly point of view; from efforts before about 1937 to observe and prescribe for the *world* to efforts after 1945 to observe the world system and to prescribe for the individual nation-state actors in the system.[26] In the 1960s much of the postwar research that is not explicitly policy-oriented is still meant to be relevant to the policy choices of national governments, but there is a renewed interest in analyzing the behavior of the community of states as a system and in describing the functions which the system performed whether or not the system as a whole had willed these functions, and whether or not there existed any world authority to act upon the prescriptive implications of the analysis.

The terminology of systems theorizing is new, and much of it is as yet painfully lacking in empirical referents. "Systematic" analysis in international relations is not, however, an invention of the past decade. A widely shared expectation that the quest for universal hegemony would not be likely to succeed and a widely shared norm that it ought not to succeed, created in the European community of nations a pattern of recurrent behavior which historians and political scientists have long described in institutional terms as the balance of power. The notion of equilibrium may be inherent in any political process, but only in the international relations of the European age of world politics does there appear to have been an often self-conscious conformity to the alleged dictates of the balance which entitles the observer to identify it as an institution. Harold Lasswell's "configurative analysis" of the 1930s is a species of what in the 1960s is called systems analysis.[27] Karl Polanyi was already, before the current focus on systems theory, describing

[26] "Interwar International Relations Research: The American Experience," *supra*, pp. 1-13.

[27] *World Politics and Personal Insecurity* (New York: McGraw-Hill, 1935).

the Europe of the balance of power as "a sub-organized system." [28] Furthermore, "the Western state system" has been part of the verbal stock in trade of the professor of international relations at least since Frederick L. Schuman's path-breaking textbook first appeared.[29] Kenneth Waltz has described a whole body of Western political theory in which the cause of war is to be found in the multiple-sovereignty system and the prescription for peace in its reform or replacement by a world government.[30] What is new is rigor in specifying a system's characteristics and an effort to exploit fully the systems-building insights of sociologists and general systems theorists. Also, as Ernst Haas has suggested, the new systems-theorizing tends to reflect physiological systems analogies rather than mechanical.

Political scientists have ranged widely in their quest for the material out of which to build new theories.[31] Thus, Charles McClelland has found inspiration in the work of Bertalanffy, the general systems theorist; and Parsons' sociology has stimulated such pioneers in international relations systems theorizing as Morton Kaplan.[32] The new breed of systems theorists is perhaps best revealed in its variety and numbers in the October, 1961 symposium issue of *World Politics,* to which eleven of them contributed.[33]

This is not the place for a critical review of the proliferating systems literature of international relations. A comparison of the work of Kaplan and Rosecrance may, however, point to a central task of theory: integration.[34] One, Kaplan, deals exclusively with systems maintenance and builds systems in terms sufficiently general that the whole experience of the Western state system, except possibly the post-World War II period, could be subsumed under one of

[28] *The Great Transformation* (New York: Farrar and Rinehart, 1944).

[29] *International Politics,* 1st ed. (New York: McGraw-Hill, 1933).

[30] *Man, the State and War* (New York: Columbia University Press, 1959). This point is made by Goodman, *op. cit.*

[31] See Charles A. McClelland, "Systems and History in International Relations," *General Systems Yearbook,* III (1958).

[32] *Systems and Process in International Politics* (New York: Wiley, 1957).

[33] Subsequently republished as Klaus Knorr and Sidney Verba, eds., *The International System: Theoretical Essays* (Princeton, N. J.: Princeton University Press, 1961). See also Jay S. Goodman, "The Concept of 'System' in International Relations Theory," *Background,* February, 1965, pp. 257-268, for a useful three-fold classification of uses of "system" in the study of international relations, viz.: system as description, system as explanation, and system as method. I have found particularly rewarding Ernst Haas' discriminating survey of systems theorizing in *Beyond the Nation-State* (Stanford, Calif.: Stanford University Press, 1964), Chap. III.

[34] Kaplan, *op. cit.,* and Richard N. Rosecrance, *Action and Reaction in World Politics* (Boston: Little, Brown, 1963).

Kaplan's six types. The other, Rosecrance, finds nine systems in the relatively recent European past, so many that his central intellectual task would seem to be to explain the succession of systems; systems that each last less than a generation hardly have time to collapse. It is, then, the dynamics of systems transformation that clamors for attention. It is not a criticism of either work to point out that it does not do something which its author makes no pretense of doing. Taken together, however, they permit one to ask how is the literature of systems maintenance and systems transformation to be integrated. If one keeps his theory of stability in one pocket and his theory of change in the other, he is prepared after the event to find in any event confirmation of *one* of his two bodies of theory.

This is not to say that the problem of integrating theories of stability and theories of change has hitherto not been appreciated. In the "configurative analysis" of Harold D. Lasswell's *World Politics and Personal Insecurity* developmental analysis and equilibrium analysis are each seen as essential halves of a whole theory.[35] Ernst Haas has addressed himself directly to this task of theory integration in *Beyond the Nation-State* and in some of his previous work.[36]

The study of state systems antecedent to our own, of subsystems in the non-European world, of theoretical constructs without reference to whether there are empirical referents for the imagined systems, of the succession of changes in the Western state system and of the great transformations of the twentieth century, all these have received increased attention in the 1960s.[37] The call for "the comparative study of multiple-sovereignty systems" and for the student of international relations "to transcend his own time and culture" seems to have been answered by both theoretical and empirical studies.[38]

---

[35] See also Carl J. Friedrich's introduction to Rosecrance, *op. cit.*

[36] See his "Dynamic Environment and Static System" in Morton A. Kaplan, ed. *The Revolution in World Politics* (New York: Wiley, 1962), pp. 267-309.

[37] In addition to works cited elsewhere in this essay, see Adda Bozeman, *Politics and Culture in International History* (Princeton, N. J.: Princeton University Press, 1960); Joel Larus, ed., *Comparative World Politics* (Belmont, Calif.: Wadsworth, 1964); and "Chandler Studies in International and Intercultural Relations," materials for the study of major transformations in the international system developed for the experimental teaching program of San Francisco State College (San Francisco: Howard Chandler, Publisher).

[38] See the concluding paragraph of William T. R. Fox and Annette B. Fox, "The Teaching of International Relations in the United States," *supra*, pp. 14-35. The call had in fact already been partly answered before the first publication of the essay. We referred to Morton Kaplan's *Systems and Process in International Politics*. In other connections, we cited Harold D. Lasswell, *World Politics and Personal Insecurity*, and Quincy Wright, *The Study of International*

F. H. Hinsley has sought to date more carefully the emergence of the syndrome of practices which are the marks of the modern state system. He thereby distinguishes between a system in which the ideal of Charlemagne, of an Emperor of the West, of unequal international relations between him and the rest, seemed natural and its successor system in which the aspirant for universal hegemony is seen as a great aggressor and equal international relations at least among the great powers is the norm.[39] Ludwig Dehio's Rankean portrayal of the parallel development and final merging of the great power system of Europe and that of the outer world was only in the 1960s brought to the attention of an English-speaking audience.[40]

Of the three major transformations of world politics in the post-World War II period—the shift from a multipolar to a bipolar power pattern and the consequent relative decline of the Western European great powers, the nuclear revolution in military technology which in the era of thermonuclear weapons has so far inhibited general war among the first-ranking powers, and the balkanization of the ex-imperial possessions—the first two had already been extensively described in the 1950s.[41] The third remains to be systematically treated. While the literature of political development and "nation-building" and of the processes of disimperialism has continued to grow, building on the sturdy foundations of Rupert Emerson's *From Empire to Nation*,[42] only a beginning has so far been made in describing systematically the political behavior of the newly created states (who now command an absolute majority in the United Nations), and hardly even that in describing systematically their foreign policy behavior, or the significance for the state system of the addition of many states who

---

Relations, whose "configurative analysis" and field theory were in their different ways pioneering efforts to open up the comparative study of multiple-sovereignty systems. Charles McClelland's first publications explicitly using general systems theory for the study of international relations had already appeared, though not in a periodical ordinarily read by the international relations scholarly community. See his "Systems and History in International Relations," *loc. cit.*

[39] *Power and the Pursuit of Peace* (Cambridge: Cambridge University Press, 1963). Garrett Mattingly had earlier, in his *Renaissance Diplomacy* (London: Jonathan Cape, 1955), made clear how inchoate was the notion of balance as a guiding principle in the North Italian city-state system.

[40] *The Precarious Balance* (New York: Knopf, 1962). Originally published in German as *Gleichgewicht oder Hegemonie* (Scherpe-Verlag Krefeld, 1948).

[41] See, for example, John Herz, *International Politics in the Atomic Age* (New York: Columbia University Press, 1959).

[42] Cambridge, Mass.: Harvard University Press, 1960.

differ markedly from both the great and small states of the pre-1939 period.[43] The 1960s, however, have seen a considerable refinement of the earlier analyses of bipolarity and the impact on world politics of the new military technology. The stabilization of the balance of terror and the rise of the Chinese People's Republic has given new relevance to non-nuclear forms of military violence and new urgency to analysis of the strains within each of the two main alliance groupings.[44]

Changes in military technology are not the only contemporary scientific and technological changes which may be transforming international relations. Caryl P. Haskins focuses on non-military developments in science and technology and their implications for the developing areas.[45] The Institute for the Study of Science in Human Affairs organized at Columbia University in 1966 will no doubt devote a significant part of its effort to similar studies.

Raymond Aron had already before 1960 established his right to be considered a foremost contributor to understanding twentieth-century changes in the state system in his *Century of Total War.*[46] Trained in the methods of German historical sociology and conversant with the whole range of American international relations studies, this French scholar-publicist's *Paix et Guerre entre les Nations* is a description and analysis of world politics of panoramic proportions.[47]

Stanley Hoffman in his volume of essays, *The State of War,*[48] asserts that "no problem today is more important for the scholar and the citizen than that of knowing to what extent the invention of nuclear weapons opened a totally new phase in history" (p. viii). He is a "transformation theorist" in the Aron tradition and his collection of essays is fittingly dedicated to Aron.

---

[43] Peter Calvocoressi, *World Order and the New States* (New York: Praeger, 1962).

[44] The organization of a Research Institute on Communist Affairs at Columbia University directed by Professor Zbigniew Brzezinski and of the Atlantic Studies program at the Council on Foreign Relations directed by H. van B. Cleveland symbolize the growing interest in studying polycentrist tendencies in a bipolar world.

[45] *The Scientific Revolution and World Politics* (New York: Harper and Row, 1964).

[46] New York: Doubleday, 1955. Available in paperback edition, Boston: Beacon Press, 1955.

[47] *Paix et Guerre* (Paris: Calmann-Lévy, 1962); also available in English translation (New York: Doubleday, 1967).

[48] New York: Praeger, 1965.

The New Actors in the Contemporary State System

The belief (and the hope) that at least the Europeanized world is entering a post-nationalist phase and that in the ex-colonial world prudent policies will produce genuine nation-states accounts for one kind of transformation study on which so much attention has been lavished that we may regard it as a separate category of contemporary research. The *dramatis personae* in the theater of world politics have been changing so rapidly—with the emergence of supranational actors in one part of the world and the balkanization of much of the rest—that studies of "political community," federation, disfederation, alliances, nation-building, political development and functional international organization have a place in the literature of international relations very much greater than even a decade ago.

New systems theory and new techniques of data management have been utilized in many of these studies. Thus Ernst Haas in *Beyond the Nation-State* embeds his careful study of functionalism and the International Labor Organization in a sophisticated re-examination of functionalist thinking, systems analysis, and integration theory. At Yale, a series of studies of integration using advanced quantitative methods have been built on the foundation laid in earlier studies of "political community" and nation-building.[49] Amitai Etzioni, a Columbia sociologist, has proposed a paradigm for the study of political unification which he has tested in a series of case studies.[50]

Just as "community-building" studies help us to understand the emergence of the role of supranational actors, "nation-building" studies do the same for the new national actors of the non-European world. Although mostly written in a comparative politics

---

[49] See especially the earlier study, made at the Center for the Study of World Political Institutions at Princeton University, by Karl W. Deutsch, Sidney A. Burrell, Robert A. Kann, Maurice Lee, Jr., Martin Lichterman, Raymond E. Lindgren, Francis L. Loewenheim and Richard W. Van Wagenen, *Political Community and the North Atlantic Area* (Princeton, N. J.: Princeton University Press, 1957). (Out of print for several years, it is in large part reprinted in *International Political Communities: an Anthology*, Garden City, N. Y.: Doubleday, 1966.) See also Deutsch's earlier *Political Community at the International Level: Problems of Definition and Measurement* (New York: Doubleday, 1954) and *Nationalism and Social Communication* (New York: Wiley, 1953). In addition to Deutsch's own writing on community formation his younger colleagues at Yale, notably Hayward R. Alker, Jr., William J. Foltz, Richard L. Merritt, Rudolph Rummel and Bruce M. Russett, have demonstrated a similar interest in a variety of monographs and journal articles. Many of these are cited in Bruce M. Russett, *Trends in World Politics.*

[50] *Political Unification* (New York: Holt, Rinehart and Winston, 1965).

rather than an international relations context, political development studies and comparative studies of new sovereignties by such men as Gabriel Almond, David Apter, James S. Coleman, Lucian W. Pye, Dankwart A. Rustow and Sidney Verba are indispensable to the student of international relations who must now deal with these new actors in world politics.[51]

Strategic Theory and National Security Policy

Although many of the studies so far described have great policy relevance, the two groups of studies which remain to be discussed are much more explicitly responsive to the need for clarifying the choices of responsible statesmen. These are studies of strategic theory and of the decision process. The former serve to improve the intellectual input in the calculating process of responsible statesmen who must select policies for a world enormously different from that of their predecessors. The latter by increasing the statesman's self-awareness of his role in critical decisions ought to decrease the chance and the importance of consequences of foreign policy choices which he had neither foreseen nor desired. Both are designed to make more rational the decisions of those who make foreign policy and national security policy.

The literature of contemporary strategic theory is almost exclusively the work of civilian strategists.[52] It grew during the 1950s, particulary at the RAND Corporation where the removal of barriers to effective collaboration between natural scientists and social scientists was identified as a problem and persistently sought and where classified information was more than usually available to its researchers on an "as-needed" basis.[53]

---

[51] See Gabriel A. Almond and James S. Coleman, eds., *The Politics of the Developing Areas* (Princeton, N. J.: Princeton University Press, 1960); Gabriel A. Almond and Sidney Verba, *The Civic Culture* (Princeton, N. J.: Princeton University Press, 1963); David Apter, *The Politics of Modernization* (Chicago: University of Chicago Press, 1965); Lucian W. Pye, *Politics, Personality and Nation-Building: Burma's Search for Identity* (New Haven: Yale University Press, 1962); and Dankwart A. Rustow, *A World of Nations: Problems of Political Modernization* (Washington: Brookings, 1967). These monographs will lead the reader to a variety of single-country studies.

[52] On the role of the civilian strategist see Bernard Brodie, "The Scientific Strategist," in Robert Gilpin and Christopher Wright, eds., *Scientists and National Policy Making* (New York: Columbia University Press, 1964), pp. 240-56. Although the scope of the survey is much broader than is comprehended by the term "strategic theory," the development of American academic strategic studies may be followed in Gene M. Lyons and Louis Morton, *School for Strategy: Education and Research in National Security Affairs* (New York: Praeger, 1965).

[53] See Bruce L. R. Smith, *The RAND Corporation* (Cambridge, Mass.: Harvard University Press, 1966).

The non-official, public analysis of strategic issues was already well under way in the 1950s.[54] By the early 1960s the flow of books on strategic theory and arms control was at flood-tide. Herman Kahn's *On Thermonuclear War*[55] and Thomas C. Schelling's *Strategy of Conflict*[56] were major contributions to the theory and the diplomacy of deterrence. The strategic debate and the concrete issues of Western policy regarding NATO were joined in Alastair Buchan's *NATO in the 1960's*[57] and in Robert E. Osgood's *NATO: The Entangling Alliance.*[58] Raymond Aron in his *The Great Debate*[59] and the Swiss journalist, Urs Schwarz, in his *American Strategy*[60] have done important jobs of synthesis for both European and American audiences.

If the first generation of civilian strategic writing was predominantly concerned with deterrence, prevention of surprise attack and avoidance of accidental thermonuclear war, a second has focused on arms control and the management of violence in less than two-way thermonuclear exchange situations. Robert Levine's *The Arms Debate,*[61] Hedley Bull's *Control of the Arms Race,*[62] and Thomas Schelling's and Morton Halperin's *Strategy and Arms Control*[63] are only three titles in an enormous literature. Halperin's *Limited War in the Nuclear Age,*[64] Herman Kahn's *On Escalation,*[65] William W. Kaufmann's *McNamara's Strategy,*[66] and Klaus Knorr's *On the Uses of Military Power in the Nuclear Age*[67] all deal in one way or another with the economical use of violence while minimizing the risk of unlimited general war. Mention should also be made

[54] See William W. Kaufmann, ed., *Military Policy and National Security* (Princeton, N. J.: Princeton University Press, 1954); the two books on limited war, Henry A. Kissinger, *Nuclear Weapons and Foreign Policy* (New York: Harper, 1957), and Robert E. Osgood, *Limited War* (Chicago: University of Chicago Press, 1957); Bernard Brodie, *Strategy in the Missile Age* (Princeton, N. J.: Princeton University Press, 1959); and Albert Wohlstetter's often reprinted "The Delicate Balance of Terror," *Foreign Affairs,* January, 1959, pp. 211-34.

[55] Princeton, N. J.: Princeton University Press, 1960. See also his *Thinking About the Unthinkable* (New York: Horizon Press, 1962).

[56] Cambridge, Mass.: Harvard University Press, 1960. Note also Professor Schelling's *Arms and Influence* (New Haven: Yale University Press, 1966).

[57] New York: Praeger, 1960; rev. ed., 1963.

[58] Chicago: University of Chicago Press, 1962.

[59] Garden City, N. Y.: Doubleday, 1965.

[60] Garden City, N. Y.: Doubleday, 1966.

[61] Cambridge, Mass.: Harvard University Press, 1963.

[62] New York: Praeger, 1965.

[63] New York: Twentieth Century Fund, 1961.

[64] New York: Wiley, 1963.

[65] New York: Praeger, 1965.

[66] New York: Harper and Row, 1964.

[67] Princeton, N. J.: Princeton University Press, 1966.

of intensified interest in guerrilla war and in non-military instruments to promote foreign policy objectives.[68]

If the development of strategic theory has broadened the base of relevant considerations in making foreign policy choices, a variety of researches offer the possibility of improving the efficiency of the policy-maker in applying available means to specified ends. My essay on the impact of Frederick S. Dunn on the American study of international relations described his pioneering research in "improved decision-making," by which he meant not decisions more in accord with his own value preferences but decisions whose consequences were more in accord with the expectations of the men making them.[69] Once the effort to deny political choice and to exorcise, or inveigh against, "politics," is given up, the decision-maker sees more clearly the values he is promoting, the calculus he is using and the role he is playing. Dunn's own *Peace-Making and the Settlement with Japan*[70] is a careful case study enriched by the author's reflective and generalizing comment. Harold Stein's *American Civil-Military Relations*[71] is a substantial casebook whose editor deliberately stops short of telling the reader what answers he should give, as he reads the successive cases, to the question "What is this a case of?" The three cases on defense budgets and national security policy described by Warner R. Schilling, Paul Y. Hammond, and Glenn H. Snyder contain a good deal of analysis of the perspectives of those contending within the American government for determining government policy in ways that importantly affected its behavior in world politics.[72] Somewhat similar efforts, to codify the behavior of particular categories of decision-makers, are those of Schilling and Gilpin with respect to scientists and of Fred C. Iklé with respect to diplomats.[73]

---

[68] On non-military instruments see, for example, George Liska, *The New Statecraft* (Chicago: University of Chicago Press, 1960); Andrew M. Scott, *The Revolution in Statecraft: Informal Penetration* (New York: Random House, 1965); and Bradford Westerfield, *Instruments of America's Foreign Policy* (New York: Crowell, 1963).

[69] "Frederick Sherwood Dunn and the American Study of International Relations," *supra*, pp. 36-56.

[70] Princeton, N. J.: Princeton University Press, 1963.

[71] University of Alabama Press, 1963.

[72] *Strategy, Politics and Defense Budgets* (New York: Columbia University Press, 1962). There are many other "image" and "perspective" analyses which might have been cited.

[73] Warner R. Schilling, "Scientists, Foreign Policy, and Politics," *American Political Science Review*, June, 1962, pp. 287-300; Robert Gilpin, *American Scientists and Nuclear Weapons* (Princeton, N. J.: Princeton University Press, 1962); and Fred C. Iklé, *How Nations Negotiate* (New York: Harper and Row, 1964). See also Harold K. Jacobson and Eric Stein, *Diplomats, Scientists and Politicians: The United States and the Nuclear Test Ban Negotiations* (Ann Arbor: University of Michigan Press, 1966).

A quite different kind of effort to improve the calculus of the decision-maker, to which reference has already been made, is the cost-benefit analysis described in Charles Hitch and Roland McKean, *Economics of Defense in the Nuclear Age,* and introduced by Hitch, as part of the McNamara revolution in Pentagon management, into the policy-making of the Department of Defense.[74] Here, as is also true in strategic theory, the analytical methods of the economist are applied to technically difficult calculations. So long as the input of a given cost-benefit analysis comprehends the full range of foreign and defense policy objectives and there is no accidental concealing of choice in the specification of benefits sought, this new form of analysis is a powerful tool in the rational selection from among policy alternatives.

Finally, such works on the politics of policy-making as *The Common Defense* by Samuel P. Huntington,[75] *Presidential Power* by Richard E. Neustadt[76] and *To Move a Nation* by Roger Hilsman[77] make more clear how the makers of foreign policy are constrained by the consensus-building necessities of domestic politics and bureaucratic organization in a pluralistic society for the makers of foreign policy. By explicitly reminding the foreign policymaker of his domestic political role, they enable him to gain greater self-awareness and thus factor in the cost of building (or eroding) the needed consensus at home in his calculation of the preferred external course of action.

What of the future? Fashions in the labels we pin on key concepts may change. "System," "decision," "conflict," "polity," "transaction" and "responsiveness" are the "in" words of the 1960s. Not every shift in the vocabulary, however, has signalled a genuine innovation in the study of international relations; nor has every innovation required its own special vocabulary. New methods are, as in the past, more likely to supplement than replace established methods. Programming the present and impending flood of data so that it can be digested by a computer will exert a salutary pressure for logical analysis. Closing the gap between abstract theory and empirical referent will test the explanatory, predictive and manipulative potentials of a given theory. A more focused effort to integrate systems maintenance and transformation theories will contribute to our understanding of ordered change and by the same

---

[74] See also Hitch, *Decision-Making for Defense* (Berkeley: University of California Press, 1965).

[75] New York: Columbia University Press, 1961.

[76] New York: John Wiley, 1960.

[77] New York: Doubleday, 1967.

token to the ordering of change. A more sophisticated comparative politics of multiple sovereignty theories will help us to understand which of the characteristics of our contemporary system are inherent in any multiple sovereignty system and perhaps the limits within which change may be ordered. In the era of the balance of terror there is bound to be a continued interest in the use of less-than-nuclear means to order that change, and the whole phenomenon (and vocabulary) of intervention calls for investigation and reassessment such as is already taking place with respect to limited war.

The sound and fury of two kinds of debate in the professional literature of international relations seem to be dying away. There are no more souls to be saved, at least among the professors of international relations, from the utopian delusions of either the internationalists or the isolationists (although the debate continues fiercely in the *public* arena as to whether the United States may not have overreached itself in *particular* foreign and military policy actions).

The alleged dichotomy between theory-oriented and policy-oriented research has been difficult to demonstrate. Debate over the merits of the two kinds of research is unenlightening. The ultimate policy relevance of theoretical understanding may not be doubted, for analyses of policy alternatives must always be informed and clarified by theory. New ways of being practical and new ways of being theoretical have continued in the last decade to emerge together. The scholars are busy on many frontiers—the refinement of concepts; the study of analytic and concrete systems and their transformations; the collection, storage and analysis of data in ways that exploit the computer revolution; the description and analysis of integrative and disintegrative processes that modify the group structure of world politics; and the improvement of the foreign policy and national security policy calculus. Except in so far as their work reflects trends general to political science as a whole, in which field "behaviorist" no longer is a fighting word, American laborers in the vineyard of international relations seem no closer to agreement on a paradigm for international relations research than were their predecessors twenty years ago.[78] This may mean, again to use Thomas Kuhn's phrase, that their study is still in its "pre-scientific" phase. Or, it may reflect the exuberant vitality and variety of a pluralistic society disposed to be generous in its allocation of resources to understanding the politics of a revolutionary world.

---

[78] For political science as a whole, see David B. Truman, "Disillusion and the prospect for an agreed paradigm.
Regeneration: The Quest for a Discipline," *American Political Science Review*, December, 1965, pp. 865-73, in which a more optimistic note is struck as to

THE AMERICAN STUDY
OF
INTERNATIONAL RELATIONS

THE AMERICAN STUDY OF INTERNATIONAL RELATIONS

Essays by

William T. R. Fox

Studies In International Affairs No. 6

Institute of International Studies
University of South Carolina
Columbia 1968

Library of Congress Catalog Card Number: 67-65726

Manufactured in the United States of America